# Pirate's Guide

### to

## Patents, Trademarks,

### and

## Copyrights

### (Insider Tactics for Beating Pirates on Their Own Terms)

### By

# David D. Winters

#### Doctor of Jurisprudence
#### (Master Pirate, Retired)

## Published by David Douglas Winters

Address inquiries to: Winters Patent Law
2277-C, Suite 237
Wilma Rudolph Blvd
Clarksville, TN 37040

Web: http://www.ipglobal.biz
Phone: 931-906-4445
eStore: https://www.createspace.com/3854608

*Library of Congress Catalog Card No. Pending*
*Library of Congress Cataloging in Publication Data:*
*Winters, David D.*
*The Pirate's Guide to Patents, Trademarks, and Copyrights*
*ISBN-13: 978-0615632001 (David Douglas Winters)*
*ISBN-10: 0615632009*

*Contributions to selected chapters by Tracy Kane, JD*
*Edited by Debbie Tipton Winters*
*Cover photo by Asa Albert Stone III aboard Cutty Sark*
*Cover art by David Douglas Winters*
*Graphics by David Douglas Winters*
*Selected illustrations contributed by Pamela Holtz*

**These are lessons pirates hope you will never learn.**

**DEDICATED TO** the successful inventors, authors, artists, and entrepreneurs whose hard earned experience and generous candor made this book possible. (You know who you are.)

**WITH CONDOLENCES TO** the innumerable scalawags, scupper suckers, and other scurvy piratical urchins who find their easy pickin's considerable shrunk because of the above.

## AUTHOR'S NOTE

Let not this writerrrr be perceived as oblivious and offendin' to some shipmates of feminine gender due to his exclusive use of masculine-like pronouns. Avast ye belly achin'. Be it known that, yer crusty scribbler *does* understand there sails female shipmates.

But allow ye that this here particular captain be of unequivocal male-like variety. When he squints at the horizon, he sees it through masculine-like peeperrrs. That's all he knows and he can't attest to nothin' more. So's I'd be suggestin' that we jettison the genderrrr-neutral malarrrkey direct off the pier. It crimps me style and yerrr readin'.

When *you* write *yerr* own scalawag's guide, as meh'be viewed through them bloodshot and booze-blurrrred eyeballs of the fearrrsome Anne Bonny herrrself, barrrge right ahead and use yerrr exclusively feminine genderrrr vocabulary. I give you my affydavy that yerrr'll get no arrrgy-barrrgy from *me*. Be that fairrr enough, shipmate?

## AND FAIR WARNIN'

Know ye that these 'ere lessons is for mere practical business suggestions not legal counsel. We makes no promise of accuracy. Some parts attempt humorous-like exaggeration to make a point. So, like any good sailor, be powerful diligent and seamanly in evaluatin' and usin' what ye derive from these pages. Apply their guidance to particular situations only at yer own risk. Any bilge rat who sez otherwise is cruisin' to get a brass belayin' pin laid between 'is mince pies.

# TABLE OF CONTENTS

# *1*

# *Introduction*

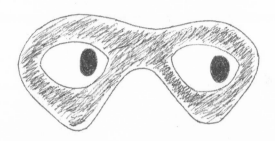

## *Pirate's Rule #1: It takes a thief to catch a thief.*

Pirates be businessmen, me hearties. Profits be their motive. Now, we dasn't advocate piracy per se. But it takes a thief to catch a thief, sez I. So, we be not reticent about purloining pages from the roving weasel's rudder books. Such secrets, as is ripped from their logs, marking rocks, shoals, ambush coves, and sheltered harbor, are what we here spreads out on the chart table.

As businessmen pirates weigh risks against benefits. A good pirate can gauge just how far the arm of the "law" will reach, where he can thumb his nose at it,[1] and how to tell if the effort is likely worth the payoff. He knows the true laws of the sea are eternal and care not a barnacle's slime for the statutory enactments of land lubber legislators. In a nutshell, he recognizes what "laws" be real laws and what "laws" be merely politician's fodder. Learn to discern this difference as pirates do or you'll be leavin' that advantage to the roving bandits.

Learn to think like a pirate. Understand how the enemy thinks, and you'll be much better prepared to fend him off or avoid him altogether. Further as a beneficial side effect, you may find your sailing becomes a fair bit smoother and the profits on your cargo more frequent and copious.

%%%%%%%%%%%%%%%%%%%%%%%%%%%%%%%%%%%%%%%%
FOOTNOTE

[1] If he still has a thumb and a nose. (Bonus Pirate's Rule: When you thumb your nose, use the arm *without* the hook.)

2

# 2

# Confessions of a Techno-Pirate

*Pirate's Rule #2: There are only two laws in this world, what a man can do, and what he can't.*[1]

3

I was a techno-pirate. I do confess it. In fact, I state this truth with some pride. Even while actively engaged in my buccaneering, I was always rather boldly up front about my undertakings. It kept things interesting.

I now relate this history because I found it useful to learn to think like a pirate. There was and is much to be learned from pirates. But like any other conscientious businessmen, pirates tend to be a bit stingy with their proprietary information.

Therefore, when it came to pirating, I had to teach myself the business. I learned by trial and error on the job, so to speak. However, few people have the necessary time or inclination for such self-education. So for those more genteel citizens, I offer some of what I learned from buccaneering.

Call it penance.

As I said, while playing the brigand, I was always pretty up front about my business. My mates and I worked on a broad scale. No surreptitious, small time, freeboot downloading, software copying, or cable TV tapping for us. The techno-pirates of my ilk were essentially blockade runners. As such, we were in the business of supplying goods not taking them. And supply the goods we did, wholesale on a scale that would give Captain Rhett Butler an inferiority complex.

What we smuggled was telecommunications. Similar outlaw bands were spread all over the world and Seven Seas privately providing high volume, high quality, low cost, telecommunications products in what was an otherwise government monopolized, low supply, poor quality, overpriced market.

This was back in the days when the US had free competition in telecommunications, but nobody else did. All other nations on this planet depended on expensive, inefficient, government-run, bureaucratic behemoths for telephone and telegraph services. The world was poised on the edge of a massive communications revolution. All it needed was a little shove to break loose the monopolies and tumble them over that edge.

We gave it the shove.

We started our melee because some of us who possessed a smidgen of law and a touch of technology had stumbled across a loophole between the two. That loophole let us bypass the "official" government monopolies and import our own free market telecommunication services.

The temptation presented by this situation was just too potentially rewarding and too easy to fulfill. We could not resist. After all, we were but violating mere arbitrary (and clearly questionable) statutes. A classic case of "malum prohibitum" (Not evil; merely prohibited.). As quoted above, from the viewpoint of a pirate, *"There are only two laws in this world, what a man can do, and what he can't."* [1] The rest are more like guidelines

It was potentially profitable, and we could do it. So we did it. As I mentioned, our activities were not universally accepted as strictly permissible.[2] But nobody could stop us.

And our efforts were fabulously successful. As is sure to happen in any free market commerce, our initial economic advantage yielded stupendous profit margins. As more and more pirates entered the fray, competition between brigands became increasingly desperate and cutthroat. This drove us to increase quality and decrease costs even more. This was good for our customers.

The monopolies hated us and battled to shut us down. But customers loved what we gave them, and they *needed* it. As dictated by the laws of supply and demand, we...and our customers...inevitably won the battles. Granted, this revolution is not yet complete. In some parts of the world it has barely started. But the outcome is not in question.

Nowadays, I am a counselor at law. Some might consider this to be a bit of an incongruous calling for a previously upright and honorable pirate. Since most of our readers have surely had their fill of lawyer jokes, we shall not further address the matter. Merely note that to defeat pirates, you must learn to think like one. Consequently, what I learned as a techno-pirate serves me well as an attorney and advisor.

Turning here to matters learned in this chapter we address one main lesson comprising three parts. The lesson addresses how to protect and profit from intellectual property (IP) while avoiding the hazardous rocks and shoals of litigation. We teach a tactic that exploits self-regulating qualities of a free market. In our postindustrial society wherein intellectual property production and export are key sources of revenue, this is a profoundly important subject.

A number of protections are well known and popularly taught, some procedural and some legal. The conventional protections are trade secrets, copyrights, trademarks, and patents.

Probably the most effective protection is secrecy. Absolute secrecy gives absolute protection against theft of IP. The problem with this method is that in many cases it is difficult to profit from a product that is totally undisclosed.[3]

Patents and copyrights are probably the best known IP protection measures. Along with trademarks, they share a disadvantage. This disadvantage is that they may require expensive legal enforcement action and assistance to exploit, for these protections are based on the power of government coercion, pure and simple. They are effective only where and as far as their supporting enforcement systems are effective. They depend upon statutes that may prove hard to police. In our world of international commerce, the long arm of the law sometimes has a short reach.

Thus, these legal protections often prove less than satisfactory. From some perspectives, they seem to be losing ground. Indeed, for many purposes, the present patent and copyright structure, and the means of enforcement, may be approaching obsolescence.

Be this as it may, the situation by no means renders intellectual property worthless, for patents, copyrights, and trademarks are not the final word. Other effective means of protection are available to augment or substitute for them. In fact, from my own days as a thimble rigger, operating on the *other* side of the law (using the term loosely), I learned that the most effective protection is tactical not legal.

One preferred tactic, essentially, is to out-compete the pirates. I call it the "Fair Fight" tactic. After all the last thing any pirate wants is a fair fight. In a fair fight, the guys in white hats have an advantage. They have access to fair profits at little legal risk. But a pirate is always in peril. He takes legal risks in hope that he will glean stupendous booty. Why would he go to all the trouble and risk of cheating just to obtain mere "fair profit"? Given the choice between a fair fight and a tactical retreat any sensible pirate will always take the coward's way out and search for easier, more profitable prey.

The "Fair Fight" tactic has three components. These are:

☠ **Quality**
☠ **Price**

and

☠ **Supply**

At first glance this looks more like the generalities of a business and marketing plan not a security system. But if these three requirements are fulfilled, no maneuvering room is left for the brigands. They are squeezed out and forced to search other waters for their booty.

Let's examine the components in greater detail to see how they work.

By the first element, "Quality," I mean an honest product. The product is "merchantable." It does what it is purported and reasonably expected to do. The buyer will not be disappointed with his purchase. He will have no cause to seek out a better replacement. If the buyer is happy with his product, one hatch whereby sea weasels might have otherwise slipped through is firmly battened down.

But if this standard is not met, an invitation to piratical invasion is, by default, extended. An opening is created that the potential smuggler can exploit legally or otherwise. If your product does not meet the quality standards demanded or expected, somebody else, legally or otherwise, will provide a product that succeeds where yours failed.

"Price" is short for "reasonable price." The buyers feel they got value for money. If they paid a modest price, they got at least a modest product. But if they paid a lot, then they got a lot.

If this standard is not met, potential customers will be dissatisfied, and demand for a better deal will emerge. Again, this is the sort of opening a roving bandit welcomes. He will offer the fairer deal that the customers crave.

"Supply" means that demand is met. Availability of the product is commensurate with the wants and needs of the buyers. If the legally legitimate purveyors do not meet mass demand for their product, pirates will likely make up for any shortfall, if they can. They will do so because it is profitable.

Using my own bonny crew's shenanigans as a case in point, we exploited failures of all three elements by a number of national telecommunications services. At that time, the necessary physical infrastructure for cheap telecommunications was already in place. Transoceanic optical cables of high digital capacity were already laid. Excess satellite channels were available at bargain basement prices.

But the bloated European bureaucracy could not bring them to fruition. The benefits did not reach the public.

European telephone service was still analog, not digital. It was expensive, of poor quality, and available only in limited quantities.

This left plenty of room for communications corsairs to undercut the abusive, but "legitimate" telecom companies in all three areas, and we did so with a vengeance. When we made our high quality product inexpensively available, the public seized upon it with true passion.

It is worth noting that no such piracy flourished in the USA. This was not because of stricter enforcement or government coercion. The US had no telecom pirates because free market competition left no weaknesses for pirates to exploit. The industry was already relatively fit and slim. It had trimmed most excess fat long before our "pirate" technology became available. So the techno-pirates went elsewhere. Like Robin Hood, they choose to plunder the rich not steal from the poor. This was not from altruism. The rich and obese simply promised better profit margins.

Another case in point was evident when the iPhone® first came out. As the more technically aware readers (we of the "techno-nerds" crowd) will recall, the iPhone® introduced as an expensive gadget of limited availability was inconveniently restricted to use on only one cell phone network.

This was less than what cell phone users had already learned to expect. It created instant demand for an equivalent system having multi-net capability. Accordingly, only a few days after the iPhone® release, pirate hackers began to convert them for use on multiple networks. Within only a few weeks, Asian techno-pirates were producing inexpensive, multi-net capable, knockoffs that also overcame a number of publicly perceived technical shortfalls of the original product.

In short, the iPhone®, introduced with much fanfare, did not meet customer expectations. It was expensive, but its performance was popularly not judged to justify its cost. Relative to demand, it was in limited supply, but quickly lost benefit of the artificially high demand resulting from this short supply. Pirates quickly picked up the slack in many markets. Very shortly, thereafter, Apple® updated the original model and rushed the next version to shop shelves, apparently to recover that slack. Eventually, Apple® found it necessary to make the phone compatible with multiple carriers.

Somebody should'a told'em earlier. The enemy offers no quarter and can be compelled to give none.[4] As counselors, our duty is to advise our clients as to viable means by which they may prevent such piracy. Again I pragmatically point out that the best prevention is a good tactical defense in depth consisting of three layers:

☠ **Offer an honest product. (Quality)**
☠ **Charge a reasonable fee. (Price), and**
☠ **Meet demand. (Supply)[5]**

Such standards mean one sort of challenge to major industry, but present a completely different obstacle to the independent entrepreneur. For the small operator, these standards present stiff challenges. The independent entrepreneur, alone in his skiff and facing a vast ocean populated by cruising corsairs, is poorly armed and engined for battle on the high seas.

Intimidating.

Yet he needs not face these challenges alone. He may join an armed convoy, so to speak, and sail with more powerful sea lords.

That is why, for those independent inventors who come to me for counsel, I always include instruction on and recommend favorite books about product licensing. The independent operator needs to understand both the advantages and the potential pitfalls of licensing.

Small or independent entrepreneurs need to understand how to use licensing and how to choose a licensing partner to strengthen their positions. A good licensing partner can provide a bulwark against bigger competitors and can also help the entrepreneur fulfill the three standards of quality, price, and supply.

The benefits are easily understood. Complex math is not, for example, required to convey the advantages of fractional royalties over undivided profits. Ten percent of a million doubloons trumps one hundred percent of ten doubloons without much explanation. Of course, the cost reduction resulting from mass production further magnifies the potential benefits of having a big partner.

But then, as any pirate can tell you, everything depends on finding a *trustworthy* cohort. Experience has shown that a number of fields of commerce may prove hazardous to a licensor's navigation.[6]

In any case, having a patent or copyright in place or applied for before opening negotiation with a potential licensee is a good business practice.[7] Your patent or copyright is the stone that tips the scales in your favor. It gives definition to and legal possession of the product you purvey. Assuming that you maintain the three "fair fight" tactical components, above, your patent or copyright gives you the advantage needed to negotiate in safety.

This is because the potential licensee knows that, although he may be bigger than you, he may not be bigger than the other potential licensees whom you will approach with your patent, trademark, or copyright documents. So, although your little skiff, alone, may not present much of a threat, the rest of the fleet that you eventually join may be formidable. Thus, the possible payback for any traitorous buccaneer who maneuvers to take your weather gauge could, indeed, be "Hell". To attack you would not be worth the risk.

That, in a nutshell, is our first lesson in how to think like a pirate…and a bit of how to talk like one. To this, I offer but one more mandatory comment. "Arrrrrgh!" (You may quote me.)

11

%%%%%%%%%%%%%%%%%%%%%%%%%%%%%%%%%%%%%
FOOT NOTES

1. Quoth, movie Pirate "Jack Sparrow" in *Pirates of the Caribbean*, a Walt Disney Pictures production.

2. Some local authorities considered our activity unlawful. But at that time, *international treaty and convention* came down squarely on our side. So knowing their claims were on legally shaky ground, the national authorities sought to stop us by *technological* means, only. They threw up technological armor. We figured out how to penetrate it. Demonstrating a basic law of combat, they lost the war, for it is a common axiom that, "In the race of bullets against armor, bullets always, ultimately, win." Code breakers always eventually defeat code makers.

3. In the case of our own telecom products, we could not avoid disclosing, or for that matter, extolling, what we did. In fact, our marketing benefited from revealing some of our clever methods. So only the most proprietary details of our operation remained hidden. To anyone with a head for technology, the general workings of our system were immediately obvious, anyway.

4. Referring again to the fictional pirate Captain Jack Sparrow, "Take all you can. Give nothing back!"

5. Note that in using this approach profits tend to be maximized by fully meeting demand, resulting in an increased sales volume with each sale generating a commensurately more modest profit margin. This is in contrast to depending on much fewer sales for the same quality goods, each sale demanding a much higher profit margin.

6. I have found that as a rule of thumb the more any industry is based on hype and volume over quality, the less trustworthy are its members. Entertainment, healthcare, and used car sales are examples that spring quickly to mind but such risk is "available where ever dreams are sold." The entertainment industry is in particular and as a matter of record not shy about embracing such culture. *"The whole music business in the United States is based on numbers, based on unit sales and not on quality. It's not based on beauty, it's based on hype and it's based on cocaine. It's based on giving presents of large packages of dollars to play records on the air."* (Frank Zappa). To this sentiment he is said to have added, perhaps apocryphally, *"The business also has an unpleasant side."* Now there was a pirate instinctively knew what he was about. (**http://www.musicbizacademy.com/knab/articles/musicquotes. htm**)

7. This is analogous to a rule taken from riverboat gamblers rather than upright, hardworking pirates. But for prudent seamen, it is valid, just the same, "Always trust the other players at your Poker table, and always cut the cards."

*This chapter is adapted with kind permission of the* Nashville Bar Journal *from an award-winning article by the same name and by the same author.*

# 3
# What's This "Intellectual Property Stuff" All About?

FIRSTEST
WITH
MOSTEST

*Pirate's Rule #3: T ain't personal.*

Learn your tools. This is an essential part of your shipboard apprenticeship. A seaman who knows not the difference between a fid and a marlinespike is unlikely to make effective use of either.

Patents, trademarks, and copyrights, and other intellectual properties (IP) are your tools; Cold, impersonal tools. They are, with the exception of trademarks, created by arbitrary statute and can be altered or dissolved as easily as they are created. Many are statutorily disfigured to the point that their original purposes are almost beyond recognition.

They were created to advance technology and knowledge. This is about business. It is nothing personal. The part about being "nothing personal" is important. Understand that *patents or copyrights are not derived from basic or inherent rights*. They are created out of thin air for the rules of a game we call "commerce."[1]

As would be true with any other game rules, we'd be silly to take them personally. Such rules may read pretty strictly, but they are arbitrary and imperfect. Many may seem unfair. As in any imperfect system, while we may quibble over details, the sensible philosophy is, "No harm, no foul."[2] So in their application, give them plenty of latitude. Get your head around this, now, and you may avoid some otherwise costly, nonproductive, and wasteful legal quarrels later. The rules are for usin' not abusin'.

On the other hand, beware that the same sorts of weasels who blatantly break these rules also apoplectically enforce them in their own favor.. Tain't personal. They treat everybody with the same arrogant attitudes; Equal opportunity abusers, methinks.

## The Philosophy of Intellectual Property

Patents and copyrights were created to provide what amounts to contracts between their owners and the public. If you create something original and useful, you can through these contracts, acquire exclusive rights to commercialize it for a limited time. In exchange for those rights, you must disclose all the details of your creation. (This is explained in the US Constitution.) That way we all can make and use it once your monopoly is expired. Everybody wins.[3] Well, at least, everybody wins so long as we stick to these basic principles. Do not assume, however, that statutes and regulations faithfully adhere to them. Legislative divergence from "the true course" can be frequent and frustrating as is noted on occasion throughout this volume. If we forget these guiding principles, everybody loses in short order.

Also, be aware that many, many lubbers banging about without direction have not acquired this simple piece of wisdom. Many legislators may be members of this large, but unfortunately uninformed, group. Do not take *their* ignorance personally, either. It is merely one of those facts with which you, now a member of the enlightened few, must struggle hereafter. Do try to teach them true doctrine should the opportunity present itself.

%%%%%%%%%%%%%%%%%%%%%%%%%%%%%%%%%%%%%%%%%

FOOTNOTES

[1] Trademarks are, as mentioned, an exception to this and generally a whole 'nother kettle of fish.

[2] A similar rule of Law, more formally ensconced is "De minimis non curat lex." (Latin, of course. Are you impressed?) Loosely translated, it means, "The law don't sweat no small stuff."

[3] "Everybody wins." This is the heart and soul of the entire proposition. The artificial and temporary rights in patents and copyrights were established to encourage folks to create useful stuff from which everybody could benefit. Intellectual property is not, nor is it intended as, a zero sum proposition. In a zero sum game, somebody wins and somebody loses. This is incompatible with the basic "everybody wins" principle for which we create intellectual property.

16

In a zero-sum game, winners gain only at the expense of somebody else. **The defining quality of zero-sum games is that they generate profit for some, but create nothing new for anybody.** Zero-sum undertakings do not create wealth. They only transfer it. Examples of zero-sum games are gambling, usury, day trading, "wealth redistribution," and various other sorts of theft and fraud. Some zero sum propositions begin corrupt. Some create corruption. All of them ultimately become corrupt•*

Unfortunately, much of our original functional copyright structure is now bent to fit the "zero-sum" mentality. For example, copyrights should be temporary. For a fair amount of time, the author or composer is awarded monopoly of his creations. After that time is expired, we all get use of them. These are merely reasonable means of encouraging fair business growth.

But so far as we can determine and predict, copyrights now endure forever. This is perversion of their purpose. And this perversion is supported by criminal penalties. By ignoring the necessity of discernible and dependable limitations on the artificial rights they create, our legislators have created a self-destructive and unsustainable system that serves only the stupidly greedy and even those, only temporarily. The addition of criminal penalties to the mix merely serves to further corrupt the entire system.

We need, in this sailor's jaded opinion, to get our eyes back on the lubber's line and correct our course. We need to get this copyright distraction off the bridge and back in the hold with the rest of our valuable cargo where it belongs. It matters not what the rest of the world thinks. You cannot win a regatta by *following* the fleet.

•*Note that taxation and fines are also zero sum propositions, and accordingly must be carefully monitored for corruption. In example, we offer that "*33½ mph on alternate Friday afternoons only,*" speed trap that caught your cousin Vinny in Crook County.

# 4
# Intellectual Property
# and the Entrepreneur

## Pirate's Rule # 4: The treasure ain't in yer chest. It's in yer head.

"...over the past decade, our clients' patents generated profits about one hundred times more frequently than the average."

Entrepreneurs are important.  They are the key to our wealth and to our economic health.  The entrepreneurs actually *generate* the precious contents of our treasure chests.  They are (forgive the cliché) the engines that pull our wealth train.  Without the entrepreneurial spirit, we become simply another once-upon-a-time-great nation.

With increasing legislation and attention concentrated on all forms of that nebulous entity termed "intellectual property," the US entrepreneur and his IP are inalienably linked.  Intellectual property can make or break him.  This places IP at the forefront.

Speaking as a lawyer and businessman, I've learned that *intellectual property is not really a matter of law.  Intellectual property is a matter of business* (recent screwball criminal copyright and trademark statutes notwithstanding).

Intellectual property rights exist, properly, only to stimulate innovation.  (They are arguably our *first and most effective* economic stimulus package.)   These rights are created specifically "to encourage progress in science and the useful arts."[1]

Their philosophical basis is a belief that good business engenders good progress.  Intellectual property has no other *raison d'etre*.  Any other touchy-feely justifications are merely straphangers swinging along for a free ride in the hold.

So as created, *intellectual property is not a component of legal tactics.  It is a component of business strategy.*  Strategy, not tactics.  This difference defines the time and level at which it must be introduced into business planning.  IP strategy must be incorporated at the earliest and highest echelons, earlier and higher than that of generalist legal counsel.

This is because, broadly speaking, lawyers are about law, not business.  Accordingly, wise businessmen compile the meat and potatoes of business plans and deals *without* the participation of rank and file general counsel.  Only after the principal points are agreed upon should such generalist lawyers be temporarily let out of their box to tidy up around the edges and engrave the corner stones. Stated succinctly in McCormack's Axiom of Division of Labor, "Lawyers *formalize* the deal. They shouldn't *do* the deal."[2] Treat this as truth, dogma, and unshakable doctrine.

However, for any business that actually *creates intellectual property*, IP attorneys are a major exception to this rule. In any such business, unified patent, trademark, and copyright counsel should be involved right from the very start of any undertaking. This is because *intellectual property is not merely about the business. It is the very basis of the business.* The business is about the intellectual property. Accordingly, IP strategy must be incorporated right smack from the laying of the keel for any associated business plan.

In large commercial concerns, this approach essentially means having intellectual property expertise solidly seated in the executive suits independent of general counsel. Establishment of an intellectual property department with a senior vice president in charge is a good organizational model. This is, in ideal example, the structure of the innovative Freescale Semi-Conductor Corporation,® wherein the Chief IP Counsel is also a Vice President. Procter & Gamble® demonstrates similar influence in that their general counsels are nation based, but the IP counsels hold positions of global authority. Below the senior IP counsel, the departments are organized according to the products associated, not according to nations or geography.[3]

So, that is ideally how gargantuan businesses may most effectively incorporate their intellectual property components. However, for small business, the attainment of early and broad incorporation of IP perspective and measures is a tougher accomplishment. Truly, the need for *early* intellectual property strategy is just as great for small entrepreneurs as it is for major corporations. This need notwithstanding, inventors and small businessmen on their first visits to my firm seldom have the vaguest understanding of how their various intellectual property rights can be combined and configured to bulwark their business structures.

As a rule, my entrepreneurial clients initially come merely seeking standalone patents, copyrights, or trademarks. These new clients usually arrive hyper-focused on one intellectual property issue, and it is often the wrong issue. They have no IP business strategy and nobody to create one. They have, by no surprise, no Intellectual Property Department.

For an entrepreneur whose entire business proposition is founded on his intellectual property, this makes for a precarious toehold in the starting block.

Recognizing and responding to this need, my firm reinvented our concept of IP practice, abandoning the "legal lawyer" approach, and embracing a broader, business strategy building, front. A generic example may serve to illustrate this difference in perspective, and the results thereof.

Let us suppose that a potential client phones, asking me to patent his newly invented super-whamodyne solar-powered Zen meter. In response, I could merely agree to play the plain vanilla Patent Attorney, prepare his naked patent application, and collect my fee.

But I don't.

Instead, I take a few moments to clarify and establish whether or not this inventor is lacking with respect to incorporation of the invention and other intellectual property into a business plan, and whether or not he knows that such may be lacking.

The answer is nearly always the same. We usually find that the entrepreneur needs significant education before understanding enough to discern what sort of IP protection and tactics are called for and why. The inventor needs to be taught how to integrate IP into his grand sailing plan.

So, we schedule a *paid* intake appointment wherein I teach this new client how we can, together, identify, weigh, cost out, and best fulfill his IP needs. Sometimes, it takes a bit of selling to get the first meeting arranged specifically for this purpose, but it is always worth the effort for both of us. And my clients consistently finish this first meeting feeling that they got much more than they paid for.

In our first session, a few brief questions reveal whether the entrepreneur has any sort of course charted that leads vaguely in the direction of success with their intellectual property. If not, we discuss the appropriateness and applicability of various intellectual property tools, associated expenses, *and the business options they create*. We discuss how IP provisions can increase or protect the value of his new technology. We explore how and what IP protection measures can get a toe in the doors of potential business investors, partners, or licensees. We define what formal IP protection measures *cannot* do. We construct theoretical time lines and project possible cash flow issues. We sketch out various practical approaches that demonstrate how IP can in practical terms be the vehicle of their success.

We do this with the view that our client's real goal is not merely to get a patent, trademark, or copyright. Our client's real goal is to make money.

When the client leaves our office after his first visit, he may not have engaged me for further services, at least not at that point. Patents, trademarks, or copyrights may not provide his best business solutions. Indeed, even if they do, the inventor may not, yet, be able to afford them. But he usually will carry away a hefty, but productive, homework assignment and a draft IP strategy. And since IP is at the heart of his contemplated business, this strategy will ultimately comprise the heart of his business plan. Once our entrepreneur possesses such basic business IP education, he is usually ready to further request and employ my services in fashioning and fine tuning his future business development.

From a small kernel such as this, great trees grow. Our clients achieve remarkable success. We know for sure that over the past decade, *our clients' patents generated profits about one hundred times more frequently than the average.*[4]

Let's quote that number again. My clients have achieved a hundredfold advantage over the average. There must be a reason. We see no likely reason other than our method.

Our comparative data comes from no less authoritative source than the United States Patent and Trademark Office (USPTO). According to that august authority, approximately one US patent out five hundred generates a profit.[5] Our clientele's profit statistics are closer to one in five. Making these numbers more remarkable, the majority of our clients are solo inventors with little or no previous experience in the world of intellectual property.

We could not know in advance that our approach would prove so successful. We did no detailed prior theoretical analysis to validate our methods. They simply made business sense. Client success, not billable hours, became our conscious target. But we've also found that client success tends to generate repeat business. So, billable hour counts tend to take care of themselves.

In additional benefit, I am convinced that our practical business cost, risk, and benefit analytical planning method leaves our clients more confident in themselves. It gives them facts and principals with which they can make better informed decisions. It gives them hard data that can help them confidently negotiate deals and contracts. It leaves them happier with their IP counsel.

Also notable is the fact that every one of my many successful clients negotiated their own license or sales agreements. Not a single one resorted to engaging a marketing or licensing agent. Each one of my successful clients boldly strode into the lion's den and secured their deals alone and without backup. I sincerely believe that most of these clients would never have dared attempt such a feat without the instruction and encouragement provided by their IP counsel (Yours Truly).

Admittedly, not all intellectual property attorneys have the necessary legal breadth, business background, or perspective to carry off the same methodology. It requires rather widely based business experience and intellectual property expertise to successfully tailor the necessary original, creative, and perhaps unorthodox means to fit small business financial resources.

These tasks involve tough choices weighing potential "bangs" against "bucks." Such things are not taught in law school. I got my own practical business experience by initiating and maintaining commercial endeavors on three continents. I've applied these lessons for my own clients for more than a decade.

In this time we learned that a Patent Attorney with business experience is the ideal combination to provide early guidance for IP based business. We assert this need of a Patent Attorney because technical comprehension sufficient to identify, understand, interpret, and classify *all* the potential intellectual property and associated measures is essential.[6] Practical business experience is the sinew that pulls the picture together. The natural creative bent of most Patent Attorneys is an additional beneficial factor.

However, in lieu of a one man show such as this, a dynamic duo of attorneys might do the trick, one having broad business knowledge, manufacturing expertise, *and practical experience* and the other qualified in *all* areas of intellectual property. To be effective, such a team must "cross pollinate," teaching each other key points of their practice areas. This approach is more expensive than engaging one lawyer, alone. But such team work would likely render their combined services more valuable than the sum of their fees.   If they can approximate the advantages my practice has managed to create for our own clients, it is worth the cost.

There may be other routes to such commercial IP success for the small entrepreneur, and others may be using them with stupendous results.   But they obviously are not exploited in great numbers.   We know this from the above quoted average rate of success to which the USPTO attests.   It remains generally dismal.

The bottom line is this.   As a means of pulling ourselves out of our present economic lethargy, our average startup business success rate must be improved.   In my law practice when assisting small entrepreneurs, a broad approach to IP, fitting it from inception, as primary component of a larger business strategy, is one key to making this success happen.   Perhaps others can learn from our experience and incorporate this lesson.   If so we all win.


%%%%%%%%%%%%%%%%%%%%%%%%%%%%%%%%%%%%

FOOTNOTES

[1]*United States Constitution*, Article 1, Section 8, Paragraph 8.

[2] McCormack, Mark H., *The Terrible Truth About Lawyers*, Beach Tree Books, William Morrow and Company, Inc., 105 Madison Ave., New York, N.Y. 10016, First Edition, 1987 by Mark H. McCormack Enterprises, Inc.

[3] Judy Jarecki-Black, PhD, Esq. and Thomas J. Kowalski, Esq. of Frommer, Lawrence and Haug, LLP, presentation for the 2009 Global IP Exchange, *"Breaking out of your Comfort Zone and Getting Involved with "Non-Traditional IP Matters"*, February 2009, Austin, Texas.

[4] Expressing this in a manner for the more statistically minded, clients whose patents are prosecuted by my firm have, and continue to, *generate profits ten thousand percent more frequently* than the average. (Yep, that number is correct. One hundred fold equals ten thousand percent.) Results like these over such a long time period are unlikely to be a mere fluke. These clients must have something special in common amongst themselves. We like to believe this "something special" is the unique preparation we give them.

[5] "There are around 1.5 million patents in effect, and in force in this country, and of those, maybe 3000 are commercially viable.", Richard Maulsby, Director of the Office of Public Affairs for the US Patent and Trademark Office, quoted in Karen E. Klein, Smart Answers, "Avoiding the Inventor's Lament," *Business Week*, November 10, 2005.

With an even more dismal view, "Experts estimate that 1 out of 5,000 inventions have gone on to successful product launches.", Williams-Harold, Bevolyn, "You've got it made! (developing invention ideas)," *Black Enterprises*, June 1, 1999.)

[6] If you cannot precisely determine the boundaries of a property, then you certainly cannot effectively protect it. Take, for example, a hypothetical licensing contract. Recall that a contract must have an identifiable subject. Lacking such a precisely defined subject, exquisitely drafted legal clauses are like finely formed arrows nocked with no clear target. All dressed up, they have nowhere to go. Beautifully ineffective.

# 5

# Mum's the Word!

## (Publicity vs Security)

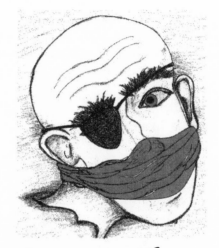

*Pirate's Rule #5:  Never miss a good chance to shut up.*

The captain of a treasure ship never brags about his cargo, nor its source, nor his destination, nor his sailing routes. (Well, not a *good* captain, anyway.) Why? Because he wants to *keep* them, matey, that's why. Otherwise, he will likely find himself reenacting the cruise of bonny ship *Hispaniola* bound for Treasure Island, packed to the gunnels with pirates even before she leaves port, even while Squire Trelawney proclaims, "Mum's the word, Ned!"[1]

Ill-considered publicity for a successful invention can be like a WANTED poster. It may please some misdirected egos. I understand Blackbeard loved WANTED posters. But in the end it bodes not well for the scalawag whose face appears on it.

The entrepreneur should consider this. Fame for the sake of fame is properly the domain only of those who deal in blue smoke and mirrors. It is probably great for narcissists of stage, screen, or politics. But for the inventor, there IS such a thing as bad publicity, ***even when it is laudatory.***

If you have a "niche market" product or invention and you manage to penetrate that market, congratulations are in order. Pat yourself on the back. Then, don't miss a good chance to clam up about it. This is not an issue of mere good manners and humility. It is an important matter of good business practice. We are not talking only about "trade secrets." I mean *all* the details of your success. Your business is *your* business, and that goes for *all* of your business.

I am sure highly publicized inventors get a real ego boost from appearing in magazines, newspapers, and inventor shows crowing about their own genius and the great sales figures or potential for their new ultra-whiz bang patent gizmos. But will it really help their bottom line? Probably not. Will it increase their risk? Very likely. What such publicity will more likely accomplish is to call attention to their perhaps previously unnoticed market, ripe for introduction of competition…or for flat out piracy.

If ego gratification is your goal, then throw caution to the wind. If you make your money on lecture tours, grandstanding is your source of profits, and your invention is merely used to make that happen, go for publicity. *But if you actually depend on the market for your invention to earn your livelihood, or hope to, then take special care as to with whom you talk and how much you tell.*

When I first started patent practice, I on occasion naively suggested to one or another *successful* client that his inventions would make great magazine copy. They usually replied by asking what useful purpose such publicity would serve. They asked, to paraphrase, "Why intentionally attract the attention of every roving buccaneer within range of twelve pound cannon shot?" (Metaphorically speaking, of course.) They preferred to stay essentially unknown to anyone outside their specific markets...and stayed successful.

Many of my clients possess enviable sales records. Some have literally thousands of distributors for their products. Some generate millions of dollars in revenue. But none of my successful inventors are bragging about their hauls. That's because they want to keep them.[2]

As my wise and successful clients have counseled their counselor (me), publicity for the mere purpose of personal notoriety should be undertaken only with great circumspection. If it does not potentially enhance your bottom line, then why take the risk? Ego gratification is alone, hardly a valid economic justification.

Many inventors or entrepreneurs whom we see dashing about granting interviews, appearing in magazine articles, and riding the show circuits probably generate more income from showmanship or book sales than from inventions. And the *primary* beneficiaries may be somebody other than themselves; Show promoters, for instance.

We do recognize that publicity used to generate commerce is usually an unavoidable cost of doing business. That is what advertising and marketing are all about. If you want your invention to sell, you must push, push, and keep pushing. Promote it without ceasing. (See Pirate's Rule #20. Hit hard. Hit fast. Hit often.)

But, target your shot. "Concentration of fire" is another principal of seaborne warfare that applies well here. A little care as to where you concentrate your marketing yields far greater return on the effort and expense than does wildly sowing your publicity cannonballs like seeds in every direction. Have a specific coherent reason for every promotion effort.

Granted, we do have inventor acquaintances who are pleased to be successful, well established, well known. Their products and names are famous in their fields. Nowadays, some of them dedicate significant time and resources to teaching the ropes to new hands on their first voyages. They become revered "Sea Daddies" mentoring entrepreneurs far and wide. Art Fry, inventor of the POST-IT NOTE®, is one admirable example. But, these folks have the advantage of overwhelming past success, branding, and solid market position. They have accrued sufficient status and resources to fend off or at least terminally intimidate most pirates of most any size. Often they are retired from the field of battle. So they can afford to teach their tactics.

Until you get your own sea legs, leave the touring, lecturing, and bragging in general, to the old hands, or to the narcissistic fops who devote their time to profiting from other inventor's dreams. For the new inventor, when it comes to publicizing your success, and the wonders of your ingenuity and genius, I offer this simple wisdom. "Mum's the word." Otherwise, somebody at the Admiral Benbow Inn (wearing an eye patch and a wooden leg?) will be taking notes not for your benefit. Your uncontrolled ego may be your only fleeting beneficiary.

Aye, Matey. Never miss a good chance to shut up![3]

%%%%%%%%%%%%%%%%%%%%%%%%%%%%%%%%%%%%%%%
FOOTNOTES

[1] *Treasure Island* by Robert Louis Stevenson

[2] See II Kings 20:12-18, Authorized Version

[3] The following should go without saying, but out of an abundance of caution, I will mention that if a patent is a possibility for your invention, you should take every precaution to keep your invention secret from the very start. The same goes, of course, for trade secrets. That means keeping a legally defendable secret from everybody. And "everybody" means "*every*body." Especially don't tell your Mamma. *Nobody* will brag to the ends of the Earth about you, your unmitigated genius, and the details of your brilliant inventions like Mamma will. So, if no patent application is yet filed, disclose nothing to nobody, no how, at no time, period. Even disclosure under an NDA ("nondisclosure agreement") should be avoided if at all possible. If you need technical assistance in developing your invention, get experienced legal advice as to how to avoid compromising your invention. At the very minimum you will need a *properly prepared* contractor's non-disclosure and non-compete agreement.

# 6

# Patent Attorneys, and Patent Agents,

Pirate's Rule #6: Patent attorneys walk on water and have big dinghies.[1]

# Patent Attorneys

Patent Attorneys are hot property. No brag; Just fact. In legal practice, patents are solely the domain of the specialist Patent Attorney, cream of the intellectual crop.

Understand, US Patent Attorneys are full-fledged attorneys in every sense.[2] Every US Patent Attorney has, effectively, at least *two* law licenses. Each must have licensure from at least one US state, and each must also pass a federal examination for admission before the US Patent Bar. The standard that must be met just to sit for this exam is rather daunting. The end result is that Patent Attorneys are essentially both lawyers and engineers. Only about three percent of US attorneys are so qualified.

Every Patent Attorney is fully licensed to practice any sort of law he cares to pursue. He can, in addition to practicing patent law, handle tax matters, write license agreements, prepare corporate papers, and if so moved, deal with the occasional speeding ticket or divorce. (This is hypothetical, of course. In reality, you will seldom find a Patent Attorney actually wandering far from his own lucrative area of specialized patent law.) The Patent Attorney is privileged to practice before the US Patent Office from within any or all fifty states no matter the state in which he resides. This is in contrast to attorneys who are *not* Patent Attorneys and are, therefore, permitted to practice any law *except* patent law and only in the particular states where licensed.

In recognition of this special status, Patent Attorneys may carry the formal "Patent Attorney" title on their business cards and stationery independently of any state levied qualifications. This is a unique and not insignificant privilege.

The process of drafting a patent application is widely recognized as the most complex legal writing task known.[3] The elite attorney who drafts your patent is termed a "patent prosecutor." But, even more elite than your "patent prosecutor" is the "litigating Patent

Attorney." This is the silver-tongued sea devil who appears in court to argue patent cases. A simple patent prosecutor may occasionally stroll across your pond just to keep in practice but litigating Patent Attorneys are generally acknowledged to maintain an altitude of at least eighteen inches above sea level at all times.

That being understood not all so called "patent litigators" are actually "litigating Patent Attorneys." They are, in fact, not necessarily Patent Attorneys at all. Mere courtroom argument is not considered "patent practice," so lawyers who *only* do courtroom work are not required to pass the Patent Bar Examination even if they are arguing patent cases. Advocates such as these are wise to engage or associate real Patent Attorneys as consultant harbor pilots, as it were, to keep them off the rocks.

So, be not deceived by creative or substitute titles that vaguely resemble the term "Patent Attorney." Check that business card. Either the bearer is flatly licensed as a "Patent Attorney," or he ain't. If you are not sure, ask without hesitation.

Given all the above, it is refreshing that when you encounter people bearing this lofty title, you will find that they tend to be really nice folks; Unassuming, but confident, clever, well read, excellent dinner conversationalists, courteous, kind to dogs, and rumored to be great lovers. I would also assert that they are invariably good looking, but the author's photograph may appear elsewhere in this book, and a good pirate knows where to stop before he is caught out. So we respectfully forgoes that particular braggadocio, shipmate.

Yet, in view of all this, you will undoubtedly not be surprised that Patent Attorneys are not cheap. In fact, at last count the highest paid lawyer in the United States was a Patent Attorney. If they were not such admirable company, we'd just term them a necessary evil. But that would be an unjust disparagement. Patent Attorneys really do tend to be worth every doubloon you dole out to them.

That said, price shopping for your Patent Attorney might prove worth the effort. Patent Attorney fee structures vary widely, with attorneys in the major cities and on the coasts commanding the highest prices (and bearing the highest overhead). But no matter where they are located, you will find that Patent Attorneys tend to be of uniformly high quality, all being subject to the same rigorous standards. Root around among the firms in the Middle West, or the South, and you may turn up a real find. Look for a small practitioner, or perhaps a semiretired one. These often provide the best value for the entrepreneur's budget.

## Patent Agents

So (might ye ask) what's the tale on them "Patent Agent" characters? What is the difference between a "Patent Attorney" and a "Patent Agent"? Well, glad you asked, sez I. Seeking an answer, perhaps we can look to good Mr. Webster. Les'see....He sez an "agent" is defined as an "attorney." Arrrrrgh. Not particularly illuminaticle. So let's look up "attorney." Well, bash me binnacle; It says an "attorney" is an "agent." It do appear that there be no difference between a "Patent Attorney" and a "Patent Agent."

But wrong'o, Snake-Wake; **This conclusion is absolutely incorrect.**[4]

We've just run up against one of the many patent law code words, over which the dictionary has no authority. The truth is this. A "Patent Agent" is a person who is licensed to practice before the US Patent Bar, but essentially nowhere else. He probably has never attended law school. He has no state issued license to practice law. He cannot write your contracts. He cannot draft your licensing agreements. He cannot file trademarks or copyrights for you.

But he can probably draft, file, and process ("prosecute") patent applications that will agreeably shiver yer timbers. This is important when one considers it with the fact that *Patent Agents are usually much less expensive than Patent Attorneys.* If all you need is a naked patent (or, at least one stripped down to its Navy issue skivvies) a good Patent Agent may be just the ticket. However, you will need some favorable fortune to find one close by. Patent Agents are rare; More rare, even, than Patent Attorneys.

This scarcity is unintentional. Patent Agents are, like patent law, a creation of statutory social engineering. Patent Agents were created to deal with the fact that "real lawyer" Patent Attorneys are unavoidably few and expensive. It was supposed that many more Patent Agents would emerge to fill the void, because the road to becoming a Patent Agent is so much shorter and less strenuous than that traversed by full-fledged Patent Attorneys. But this approach did not pan out as expected.

The reality is that very few Patent Agents are, or ever were, available for private hire. It appears that most are employed in-house by large corporations, or as assistants to Patent Attorneys in law firms. Patent Attorney numbers far surpass those of Patent Agents. You might ask, "Why is this?" And I will answer.

"I don't know."

Haven't a bloomin' clue.

If you figure it out, do write and enlighten me on the issue.

Still, by all means, if a Patent Agent can do the job you need done, search one out. However, remain aware that a US Patent *Agent* cannot offer services in the full range of intellectual property matters in the manner that a US Patent *Attorney* can provide. This full range of services is necessary to give the entrepreneur well rounded and complete support. It is important.

## Outing Their Little Secret

You should know an innocent little secret shared by Patent Attorneys and Patent Agents. The secret is that they are invariably closet inventors. They do not merely describe inventions in patent applications. They contribute to them. This is good. Any Patent Attorney worth his hardtack helps his client define additional forms of his invention. This is an important function. But shipmate, it is also inventing, pure and simple. This presents a bit of a technical problem.

It creates a legal conflict within the arbitrary statutes and regulations of patent law.[5] The problem situation is in a nutshell;

> ☠ Statutes require all contributing inventors to be listed on any given patent application.

> ☠ Patent Attorneys as a matter of course contribute to their client's inventions, so theoretically they must be listed as inventors on many patent applications.

> ☠ As a matter of ethics, but contrary to the literal reading of the above regulations, Patent Attorneys should NOT be routinely listed as inventors on their client's applications. Such self-serving conduct is rightly frowned upon.

How do patent attorneys deal with this conflict? We adhere to the tried and true tradition of putting the client's best interests first. We look upon the matter with Admiral Nelson's blind eye. We exercise that higher form of obedience which requires us to do what the Imperious Leaders would have directed had they known what they were talking about.

In other words, we *refrain* from listing Patent Attorneys as inventors on the patents they prepare. We do not consider them to be inventive contributors. (I doubt that you will ever face this problem, but if your patent attorney proposes to list himself as an inventor on your patent, point out this little issue to him.)

So when you find your Patent Attorney suggesting new, clever, or innovative ways to accomplish your invention, just smile gratefully, accept his brilliant contribution, and feign that, all along, it was exactly what you intended to include.  In fact, if your attorney suggests new ways that appear *not* particularly clever or innovative, accept those, too.  He is probably just re-enforcing the stem, keel, and bulwarks of your patent protection, using complex below deck structures not apparent to you, nor to others not cognizant of the practitioner's art.  That is all part of his job, confidentially speaking.

%%%%%%%%%%%%%%%%%%%%%%%%%%%%%%%%%%%%%%%

FOOTNOTES

[1] *Dinghies: Small open boats carried as tenders, lifeboats, or pleasure craft on larger vessels.*  (These are normal equipage for both pirates and affluent Patent Attorney yachtsmen, many of whom may be a *little* dingy, sez I.)

[2] This is in contrast to "Patent Attorneys" of, for instance, the United Kingdom, who are essentially the equivalent of US Patent Agents and, also in contrast to US "Intellectual Property Attorneys" who usually are *not* licensed as Patent Attorneys.  Because the "Patent Attorney" title is rather prestigious, the term "Intellectual Property Attorney" is usually used only by US lawyers who do not possess the qualifications required to practice patent law before the Patent Office, but still specialize in non-patent fields of intellectual property law, such as trademark or copyright, or perhaps intellectual property litigation.

That given, attorneys hired by major firms for any type of "IP" practice tend to be a rather select group.  The competition is tough.  Apparently, many starry-eyed young attorneys are attracted to Intellectual Property law practice imagining it a glamorous field in which one routinely hobnobs with celebrities.  So the ones who actually make the cut are necessarily of the sharper variety.

[3] Well it's the most complex *legitimate* task anyway. We decline to include for consideration those disastrous Wall Street generated monstrosities termed "mortgage backed securities."

[4] Take this however as a profoundly important lesson. In the world of patent documents, innocuous, unassuming, apparently harmless words become sneaky and deceitful carriers of special meanings and nuances known only to those initiated into their mysteries. So, beware the words of a patent document. They may not mean what they seem to mean. In the patent world, we begin by interpreting patent terms in accordance with the dictates of old Samuel Johnson's dictionary, which preceded Webster by a good cable length. Additionally, many terms have, in the ensuing centuries, further evolved at a rate that that would amaze even the most rabid Darwinian. These days, much patent generated terminology can be found in *no* dictionary. Compounding this progression, Patent Attorneys are the only attorneys permitted to be their own lexicographers. It has reached the point that Web sites are established for the express purpose of allowing patent attorneys to perform statistical word studies of technical terminology and court recognized meanings thereof. What does any particular term mean in a patent document? Only your *Patent* Attorney has a clue. Do not trust the opinion of any other sort of lawyer in this.

[5] To gain a greater understanding of this, allow me to recommend a book, *Excellence of The Common Law*, a hefty volume penned by my infinitely more illustrious, rabble rousing younger brother, Brent A. Winters, Esq.. Published by Mountain Press, 2008, ISBN: 09765520-0-0

# 7
# Trade Secrets

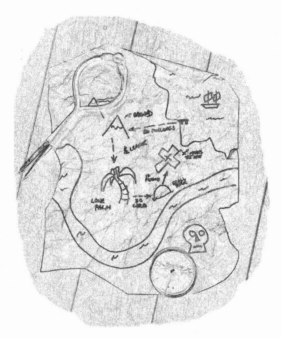

*Pirate's Rule #7: Dead men tell no tales.*[1]

*The rest are natural blabbermouths.*

A ***trade secret*** is valuable business information, such as facts concerning a proprietary process or device, or a compilation of information, like, say, customer lists, not generally known or reasonably ascertainable by outsiders. For example, if you had a treasure map, you should consider it a trade secret and protect it as such. Trade secrets can be important to your business and may be important enough to affect national security. This is nothing new. As a case-in-point, mere knowledge of iron smelting was recognized as a rather significant national security secret thousands of years ago. (See I Samuel 13:19.) I suppose the Greek gods essentially considered fire a trade secret. Its theft certainly made them cranky.

A properly protected trade secret enjoys special legal status under federal statutes and also under statutes of many states. Even if a trade secret becomes wrongfully compromised, it may still be legally protected if it was and continues to be treated with due diligence by its rightful owner. But recognize that "due diligence" means *formal, methodical security measures*. It means locked file cabinets, encrypted files, restricted access, and nondisclosure agreements for employees and others who receive given information access.

However, tactically speaking, it is better to apply trade secret security at a higher level than mere protection of contents. The wise tactician avoids letting anyone know that any secrets exist, at all.

Years ago, while I regularly worked with or in spite of various mysterious agencies all of whom appeared to be obsessed with having three-letter initials, I picked up a number of practical security practices. For one, I learned that the best communications security comes not from communications codes or encryption. The best communications security comes from hiding your communications entirely.[2]

If no one knows about your communications, no one will try to intercept or break them. Likewise, my submarine boating buddies of the "silent service"[3] know that it is better to be always submerged undetected than merely disguised or ready to hide.

Trade secrets work the same way. Don't brag about 'em. Don't talk about 'em. Avoid even acknowledging their existence. Be aware that when you hear somebody touting that his product employs some special secret formula or process, either it's a load of hype, or that advertiser is begging for a nasty infestation of corporate espionage.

If you really want to protect your secrets, avoid revealing that you have secrets to protect in the first place.[4]

%%%%%%%%%%%%%%%%%%%%%%%%%%%%%%%%%%%%%%

FOOTNOTES

[1] This is the pirate's version of *Poor Richard's Almanac* more socially acceptable observation that, "Three people can keep a secret if two of them are dead."

[2] Well, not to put too fine a point on it, the best communications security is no communications at all. But that may rather defeat the greater purpose of the security.

[3] A.k.a., "Sewer Pipe Sailors."

[4] Extending this principal in increasingly sophisticated tactics to distract the competition, you can attract attention to misleading information and at the same time make it more credible by showy attempts to hide it. For instance, broadcast a meaningless coded signal. It might be only gobblety-gook, but you can bet the bad guys will take notice, and LOTS of assets will be concentrated on trying to break the code.

Referring to a recent corporate espionage movie titled *Duplicity*,[*] this sort of tactic was brilliantly employed by the plot's ultimate victor. He created a fake trade secret and used it to lure his opponent into defeat. But such finely tuned tactical psychological maneuvering is certainly beyond the reach of anybody I know in the real world. That's my story, and I am sticking to it.

[*] Starring Julia Roberts and Clive Owen. Golden Globe nominee. Great characters. My kind of plot; Not merely tangled, but twisted, beat on rocks, run through a wringer, and hung out to flap in the salty sea breeze. Not for kids, though.

# 8

## *Patents*

## *Pirate's Rule #8 : A patent is merely a hunting license.*

"A patent is merely a hunting license; No more, no less." I assert this repeatedly, but only because it is extremely important to understand. A patent gives you the right to search out and bag infringers. For so long as your patent is effective, you have the sole right to prevent anyone else from making, using, or selling your patented invention. Anybody who does so without your permission is fair game.

But of course, just like in the case of a hunting (or fishing) license, these rights are valid only in the territory where the patent is effective. A Tennessee hunting license is worthless in Nevada. Analogously a US patent gives you rights over your invention *only in the US.* (Patents are issued only at the federal level.)

If you have a US patent:

☠ Nobody else has the right to make your invention in the USA unless you give or sell that right to them.

☠ Nobody else has the right to sell your invention in the USA unless you give or sell that right to them.

☠ Nobody else has the right to use your invention in the USA unless you give or sell that right to them.

So what happens if you have a US patent, and somebody starts manufacturing your product in, for instance, Timbuktu, Timbukthree, or Zamboanga (not in the US)? The short answer is, "Nothing happens."

So what happens if that manufacturer sells your product in those countries, or worse, exports it to even more other countries (not the US)? The short answer remains, "Nothing happens."

So what happens if that manufacturer exports your product to the United States? The short answer is, "Nothing happens." *But plenty can happen,* if you make it so. The US is your personal territory. Importation of your invention into the US is invasion of your territory. In such an event, your patent also becomes your weapon to repel boarders. Be ready to use it. That is what it is for. If you do nothing to defend your patent, nobody else will. Unlike the case of copyrights, there is no provision for enforcing patent rights under criminal statutes. (This gives us a hint of where our legislative priorities are.) And, unlike the situation with copyrights, if you do not defend your patent, *you lose the right to do so*.

Whatever the limitations on your territory, you have the right to stop anybody who violates it. The emphasis here is on the word "you." Unless you sell, loan, or license rights to your invention, the responsibility for finding and stopping infringers lies exclusively on your solitary shoulders. The Patent Office will not assist in this job, and the task is not cheap or easy. (With respect to this, refer to Chapter 2 where we succinctly address the advantages of licensing.)

Of course, if you have patents in every nation on the planet, your rights can, theoretically, be enforced in every nation on the planet. It is *all* your territory. But matey, *nobody* gets patents in every nation on the planet. And even if they did, enforcement would be a nightmare. (See the later chapter on "Boxing the Compass, the Inventor's MBA.) So we shall assume that your patent territory has, indeed, some limitations.

In pursuit of your enforcement responsibility, it is handy to know that if you find a States-side merchant selling or importing an infringing product, you can sue that merchant without going after the manufacturer or seller, overseas, or even out of state. Should you sue the seller, the foreign manufacturer or seller must "belly up" and defend against the suit in the USA, or accept a default judgment against them. Foreign infringers forced into US courts are at quite a disadvantage. The disadvantage may be so great that they give up without a fight. So even if you do not collect any sort of financial remedy, the infringing activity may be curtailed.

To gather essential data on infringers engaged in illegal importation, you can order a "customs survey" for a very reasonable fee. This can produce valuable information as to who your infringers are, and where they are selling. It also greatly inconveniences infringing importers, putting a kink in their business flow. This is a nice side benefit. Check online with the US Commissioner of Customs for details.

Once infringing distributors, retailers, wholesalers, importers, or manufacturers are identified, they can be sued in US Federal Court, or a complaint can be filed with the International Trade Commission. Neither of these options is simple or inexpensive, however. Still, if your case is a good one, some law firms will litigate on a contingency fee basis. If you win, they get paid. If you do not win, you owe nothing. Alternatively, you can buy litigation insurance from a number of sources. Search online for companies offering "intellectual property insurance."

But before you embark on the stormy seas of litigation, engage a Patent Attorney to analyze and confirm the suspected infringement. If he agrees that infringement is underway, a simple letter to the infringer may fix the problem.

Not all infringers are aware of their offenses. Not all infringers continue infringing once they learn that's what they are doing. In serving my own clients, I have found that a firm letter to the offender often does the trick. Occasionally, it produces a pleasant license deal for my client. Honest businessmen usually have enough to worry about without adding patent litigation to their burdens.

Of course, not all businessmen are honest. But as discussed in Chapter 2, "Confessions of a Techno-Pirate," the dishonest ones, the sea bandits poised just over the horizon, are generally not interested in any quarry that offers a fight, and has the guns to do so. They like their opponents weak, overwhelmed, or held at a safe range. No weak points; No pirates. If you adjust your course and armaments as taught herein, you may drive off the infringers without a fight. If you do not, then draw your sword and prepare to repel boarders!

# Utility Patents

A Utility Patent is a patent on *how something works*. An invention's appearance is of no consequence to a Utility Patent. The document contains a specification, drawings, and claims. The specification and drawings lay out a broad description of the invention. But the heart of a utility patent is its excruciatingly exact *claims*. Utility patents and the claims therein are the most complex and sophisticated textual compositions known to our legal system. Each is replete with specialized "terms of art" having meanings known only to the initiated.

To more specifically address the contents, if you had a utility patent for a muzzle loaded swivel gun, the patent would detail each component of the lock, stock and barrel and the functions thereof. It would explain various different versions of the mechanics. It would discuss the procedures followed in locking, loading, aiming, and firing the weapon. It would, all in all, teach the reader the art of building and using a muzzle loading swivel gun. This is the essential function of any utility patent.

# Design Patents

A Design Patent is a patent on *how something looks*. It is a blood cousin of "registered industrial designs" recognized elsewhere in the world. How an invention functions is of no consequence to a Design Patent. The heart of a Design Patent is its *drawings*. These must be precise, detailed, and prepared according to largely counterintuitive rules established by the Patent Office. A Design Patent for your muzzle loaded swivel gun would contain several drawings (not photographs) of the weapon, and a single textual assertion that the drawings are a complete expression of what the inventor claims as his invention.

Strictly speaking, Design Patents exist to protect ornamental creations. However, it is a recognized principle of law that, "Beauty is in the eye of the beholder." So if I, for example, file a Design Patent Application on a new design for a septic tank, no examiner is likely to reject it on grounds of failure to ornament. Sometimes this overlap or loophole can be quite valuable. Some simple inventions simply *must* look the way they look to be what they are, even if that "look" is wholly ornamental[1]. In cases such as those, design patents may provide patent protection when no other protection is vaguely available. Many authors and pundits summarily discount Design Patents as a waste of money. But such a shallow, blunderbuss approach summarily forfeits valuable, tried-and-true tactical options.

In illustration, we refer to my favorite antique airplane.[2] While researching her history, I found that the propeller for my darlin' airship was successfully protected by a Design Patent, not a by Utility Patent. Now, when you consider this, it makes perfect sense. A propeller is an excellent example of something that *must* look how it looks to be what it is. But it is also inherently beautiful. From a utilitarian point of view, propellers had been invented long before this particular model was conceived. But from an ornamental point of view, my plane's propeller design was unique. It *looked* different from any other. It had a unique appearance. As to the question of how much of that appearance was functional and how much was ornamental, the balance is not easily quantified. A Utility Patent would have been difficult if not impossible, to acquire. But a design patent to protect this unique quality was quite realistically achievable. It was just what the ship's surgeon ordered.

Also not, however, that the inventor was also the original manufacturer. He might have encountered obstacles to convincing a potential licensee of the viability of his patent, had he tried to sell it. Yet, such obstacles would be more due to the lack of perception on the part of the buyer's attorneys than to actual weakness of the patent itself. This is an example of practical, rather than theoretical, practice, a triumph of art over science (for those who properly understand the difference). It was a good patent because it *worked*. T'is a fool's errand to argue with success. If it works in fact, who cares whether it works in theory?

## Plant Patents

A plant patent is creates a temporary monopoly for creators of new, asexually (sounds boring) produced plant species. It deals with matters known internationally as "plant breeders rights" or "PBR",[3] (also known as "Plant Variety Rights"). In actual application, plant patent provisions and protections extend even to the accidental propagation of plant pollen on the four winds.

For example, if the farm next to you grows new plant breeds for seed production, and their pollen blows over the fence and pollinates, or contaminates, your own crops, you may find yourself restricted as to how, where, and for what you may sell or use your own harvest. You could, in fact, find yourself a defendant in a patent infringement suit.[4] I do not assert that this is fair. I merely state the factual situation. Remember I pointed out in Chapter 3 that the rules of intellectual property are arbitrary and may be flatly unfair. That is simply the way legislative social and economic engineering tends to degenerate.

## Statutory Invention Registration

Statutory Invention Registration ("SIR") is a little known tactical tool of purely defensive nature. Think of it as a shield, not a cutlass. It begins with all the same components of (and essentially the same filing expenses as) a patent application. It is also published by the USPTO, just like a patent application for the entire world to see. But unlike a patent, it does not prohibit others from making, using, or selling its subject invention(s). However, it should prevent anyone else from patenting the invention(s) it already covers. "Anyone" in this case, includes the inventor who submitted the SIR.

So be careful. *Anything* that happens to be contained in an SIR, even peripherally, becomes unpatentable, even if it is not the main subject of the document.

If you are an inventor or research organization who seeks no direct profit from your inventions, but wants simply to have recognition for them, and wants to make a gift of them to the world, an SIR should do the trick. Your SIR will ensure that you are entitled to not a single copper in royalties.

Also understand that, as is also true of any patent, the actual manufacture, sale, or use of the invention claimed therein may yet infringe a different patent. This is worth repeating. ***Even though you actually possess an SIR or a patent for your invention, if you actually practice your new technology, you still may be infringing somebody else's patent.*** This is because although your claimed invention may indeed, be new, it may also contain or be integral to a different invention that is subject of an entirely different patent. So to legally make, sell, or use your invention, you may, first, need permission or license from the owner of the other patent.

For example, let us imagine that somebody else owns the patent on all bicycles. Let also us imagine that you invented a new type of bicycle seat. Now, you may get a patent or SIR for your new bicycle seat design. But you cannot manufacture it on a bicycle unless you get permission or license from the owner of the bicycle patent. See how it works?

Carrying this hypothetical a bit further, let us suppose that your new patented bicycle seat is so great an improvement over the old ones that nobody wants a bicycle without your seat. This may put you in a strong position to sell the bicycle manufacturer a license for your patent so he can make and use your seats. Or, if *you* want to manufacture bikes, this may put you in a good position for *cross licensing*. In a cross license, you give the bike maker a license to use your seat patent, and, in exchange, he gives you a license to use his bike patent.

On the other hand, if you have an SIR instead of a patent, you have no leverage for getting a cross license because the bike manufacturer can use your invention for free, anyway.

Now, given all that, the Statutory Invention Registration's days are coming to an end. The option to file an SIR goes away under the latest patent legislation. However as a substitute procedure, simply filing a patent application, and then abandoning it after it is published should still accomplish essentially the same function.

%%%%%%%%%%%%%%%%%%%%%%%%%%%%%%%%%%%%%
FOOTNOTES

[1] In theory, this makes them ineligible for design patents. But in reality, design patents are constantly, and successfully, employed to deal with such situations.

[2] A 1946 Ercoupe, the most futuristic aircraft of her day. See Appendix III *Example Protections Tactically Employed.*

[3] In deference to fellow sailors, we note that PBR is also an abbreviation for "Patrol Boat, River," a brown water assignment that tended to produce an uncomfortably high number of awards for valor, all legitimate.

[4] See *Monsanto Canada Inc. v. Schmeiser* 1 S.C.R. 902, 2004 SCC 34 [2004].

# 9
# Provisional Patent Applications

## Pirate's Rule #9: <u>Nobody</u> has a Provisional Patent.

*(You bet'cher flat hat!)*

There are three important things to remember about Provisional Patent Applications:

- ☠ There is no such thing as a "Provisional Patent."
- ☠ There is no such thing as a "Provisional Patent."

and

- ☠ There is NO SUCH THING AS A "PROVISIONAL PATENT."

Despite innumerable Internet ads that promise "Provisional Patents" for bargain basement prices, nobody has, nor ever had, nor can obtain, a "Provisional Patent." Period, full stop, cross my heart, and hope to doo-doo in my best flat hat.

Congress did, some years ago, create a creature called a *Provisional Patent Application ("PPA")*. This is a *provisional* application for a *regular* patent. It is *not* an application for a "provisional patent." (See 1 through 3, above.) The idea was to provide a low cost means for poor inventors to get their toes in the door of the patent application process.

The plan did not work out particularly well. A valid patent application must meet certain minimum standards. The courts have found that many Provisional Patent Applications, being of a skeletal nature, do not meet those standards. To get a Provisional Application drafted up to snuff, you can expect to pay about the same thing as you would pay for a full-up regular patent application. That's a long run for a short slide.

Now, I admit that on occasions, due to one or another time crunch, I have submitted Provisional Patent Applications for my clients. But I did so with my clients fully aware that the document would be of limited potential. We did it because a PPA was all time would allow.

A Provisional Application merely serves as a place marker. It provides, *if* properly drafted, a priority date for your follow on Regular Patent Application, which must be filed within a year if that priority date is to be preserved. With a PPA filed, you can legally mark your invention "Patent Pending."

In my opinion, the greatest value of the PPA is that the solo inventor might be able to prepare one for himself. With proper guidance, careful attention, and minimal expense, you can draft and file your own provisional application. Books and software are available to assist in this task. Allow, mate, that the resultant application might be worth less than a pasteboard dogging wrench. But if you cannot afford anything else, a "Do-It-Yourself" Provisional Patent Application may be better than nothing. *Maybe.* So depend on one only with full knowledge of the risk involved.

If you have an ongoing invention process, regularly updated PPA's can ensure that you have the earliest possible filing priority date for your most recent version of the invention. But remember, your PPA will never mature into a patent. Never. In fact, your PPA will never even get examined. When it arrives at the Patent Office, the technical shop stamps it, scans it, records it, sends you a receipt, and promptly forgets the whole thing. The only person likely to ever look at your PPA is the enemy who wants to invalidate, or otherwise break, your associated patent. You can bet *he* will go over your PPA with a fine toothed comb. But nobody else really cares.

So be cautious when trusting in a provisional patent application. Use it as a last resort, only. And, remember, "There ain't no such thing as a Provisional Patent."

# 10

# 𝒫atent 𝒮earches

## 𝒫irate's ℛule 10: 𝒜 patent search is a tool. 𝒟o not scrimp on your tools.

A good patentability search is a valuable navigational tool. A poor one is a hazard to navigation.

Why do a patent search? Well, first, a patentability search can help establish whether your "invention" has already been invented. Once invented, always invented, whether patented or not. If your supposedly new device was originally protected by a patent, say, over a century ago, that patent is therefore long expired. But the invention cannot be patented again.[1] It was already invented. For the cost of a patent search, you can learn enough to avoid the much greater cost of a wasted patent application. Consider it insurance.

Also a good patentability search can give an excellent picture of what competition your invention may face, and can chart the various preceding patent "minefields" that you must navigate in order to get your own patent allowed. Consider it an aid to navigation.

There are many levels of products calling themselves "Patent Searches." For a couple of hundred dollars, you can probably order one such product, of questionable validity, that amounts to no more than a stack of patents and an invoice. The analysis is left up to you. This is of little use to the average person, for interpretation of the findings is ninety percent of the job. If you are not a Patent Attorney or Patent Agent, you do not have the necessary expertise to analyze and interpret the findings.

One step up from that product is a package that includes a similar stack of patents, but also includes a terse letter that says, essentially, "We [do *or* do not] think your invention is patentable." Some respected Patent Attorneys or Patent Agents turn out such products. This still leaves much to be desired.

Make it clear that the product you seek includes a detailed letter saying, *"We searched the below listed sources. Our discoveries are individually analyzed and their likely impacts on the patentability of your invention are presented herein."* The search report should address what was found, item by item.

With research like that in hand, you can make an informed decision as to what next step to take (or not take), what your market environment may be like, and what challenges your own patent application will face. Furthermore, the results of your patent search can be used by your patent attorney to write a more formidable patent application. By referring to the findings he can plot courses around whatever obstacles the search reveals.

This sort of search will cost, at a minimum, several hundred dollars and may cost thousands, depending on the technology addressed. But it is almost always a very wise investment.

%%%%%%%%%%%%%%%%%%%%%%%%%%%%%%%%%%%%%%%%%
FOOTNOTE

[1] This frequently happens. On my desk I have a copy of a patent awarded for a rocket plane designed a year before the Wright brothers managed to get their Wright Flyer off the ground. This same patented super-stratospheric plane, retrorockets and all, was finally flown (and unceremoniously crashed) by Colonel Chuck Yeager in 1963, long after the patent expired. (Patent no.710,266, by one Theodore Gibbon, a resident of Clarksville, Tennessee.)

# 11

## *Trademarks*

# TM ® SM

*Pirate's Rule# 11: Trademarks don't need no stinkin' registration. (But registration is cheaper than litigation.)*

*"He.... who filches my good name... makes me poor, indeed." (Othello,* Act 3, Scene 3*)*

Your trademark is your good name.  It is the bearer of your reputation.  Your exclusive right to your trademark, your rightful commercial name, is independent of any and all legislative drivel.

The trademark is the only true intellectual property.  The rest are mere statutory fictions.  The right to your trademark, like the right to your good reputation, is not created by legislators.  It predates any statutory enactments.  Like any other true property, it cannot be multiplied.  Only one person can fully possess it at one time.  That is to say, at any given instant, in any given commercial

59

field, it is diminished if used by more than one person. If more than one person shares true property, each gets something less than the whole. Trademarks work that way.

To better understand this, contrast it with, for example, a musical piece that can be sung, whistled, played, hummed through a kazoo, or otherwise shared and reproduced by unlimited millions simultaneously without diminishing it. This is a quality incompatible with being genuine property. Thus, so called property rights in music are legal fictions created by legislation only. This is clearly different from the basic and inherent right to the true property of your trademark.

Like any other true property, your trademark can be bought or sold. It has value. If you sell it, give it up, or lose it, then you cannot use it any more unless you get it back. But, like any other piece of fragile property, when and if it is recovered, it may not be in the same pristine condition it previously enjoyed.

Since your trademark has definite but fragile value, you should protect it. If you do not protect it, you will lose it. For somebody else to trade under your mark is like having somebody else borrow money against your credit reputation. It cannot be good.

And if you trade under a mark belonging to someone else, you can expect an understandably unpleasant response from the legitimate owner, for you would be infringing for a free ride on his hard earned reputation.

For centuries, the accepted standard for deciding trademark infringement issues has been "likelihood of confusion." If a new trademark on a product was likely to be confused with an old mark belonging to someone else, then it infringed the previously established mark. The idea was to ensure that the buyer could discern the sources of the products he bought. If good Captain Bligh bought a bailing bucket that said it was made by the JACK AND

JILL PAIL COMPANY, he could bank on getting a bucket of the same quality as this last purchase from the same company.

But if some other scalawag started selling third rate scuttlebutts under the same name, thereby capitalizing on Jack and Jill's good reputation, marketplace trust would go flying out the nearest porthole. And the legitimate JACK AND JILL would lose reputation and lose business. So exclusive trademarks, early on, became a justly recognized right.

It is worth repeating that this was long before creation of any sort of trademark legislation. It is worth repeating that trademark rights were not created by Congress or any other legislature. Trademark rights were long ago recognized by the Common Law. And they are recognized under our Common Law today.

It is, of course, common knowledge that the Common Law is a direct and undisputed progeny of common sense. No statute was ever required to tell judges that it is wrongful to unjustly trade on the business reputation and good name of a competitor. This was just common sense then, and it is common sense, now.

This well settled common sense has long held true for everybody except of course for a remarkable number of recent legislators functioning under the guise of "lawmakers," a title that even Moses refrained from assuming. This bit of silliness is further discussed in the next chapter, *What is a Famous Trademark?*

Given that a Common Law trademark is not "granted" by the government, it is not acquired by submitting an application form. You create your trademark by using it. It does not exist until you actually slap it on a product, and put that product on the market. Your trademark is born at that moment, and it does not die until you stop using it. Period. All you need to create and possess a trademark under the Common Law is to choose it and use it.[1] (This is assuming, of course, that you choose one that is in fact available and not in use by somebody else.)

We grant that you can apply to have your trademark registered with the government. You can pay fees to keep it listed as "alive." If you stop paying your trademark dues, the Trademark Office will pronounce it "dead." But so far as the courts are concerned, all such status awarded by the Trademark Office is, for want of a better term, merely advisory. The court is the final arbiter, not the Trademark Office.

Now, given that you clearly understand this basic underlying truth, you will probably ask yourself if you would better forego the trouble and expense of formal registrations for you trademark.

The answer is, "No."

Choose a clever trademark mark; Something short, sweet, melodic and memorable. Make sure it is available. Then, use it, use it, use it. And do get it registered.

By all means, do register your trademark. Do it at both the state and federal levels, simultaneously. State registration is effective, and comparatively quick, easy, and cheap. Do it for that reason. Federal trademark registration is *not* quick, easy, or cheap. But it is very powerful. Do it for that reason.

Trademark registration serves a number of practical purposes. First and foremost, registration establishes a "presumption of validity" for your mark. (Not putting too fine a point on it, it is more precisely a "rebuttable presumption of validity." We lawyers do love such talk.) This means that the government attests that your chosen mark has already been checked out published, and approved. Objections (if any) were dealt with. Your chosen mark was pronounced available, and formally registered as your rightful property in the opinion of the Trademark Office.

The courts will generally presume validity of any mark so registered. To defeat it, a challenger must successfully accomplish the expensive and tedious task of "rebutting" that presumption. So should your trademark be challenged or infringed, previous registration can save you loads of money, time, and trouble. Believe me, when you consider the potential expense of a trademark suit, registration looks like a real bargain.

A trademark can also give you an important "leg up" in the marketplace, even in the absence of patent protection for your product. If you produce a valuable product, charge a fair price, and meet demand, it has a good chance of flying when you push it out of the nest. Your trademark is the wing under which you launch it.

So when you place your valuable product before the public, identify it, consistently and categorically, with your trademark. Your goal is to be the "firstest with the mostest." When people think of your superior product, you want your trademark to automatically leap to their minds. When they ask for your product, you want them to automatically tend to refer to it by your trademark, not by a generic or functional description.

Other attorneys may advise you to avoid permitting your mark to be used as a generic term, of itself. You can lose rights to the mark should such usage become the norm. This was, for instance, the fate of "aspirin." The term was originally a trademark, but is now freely used by everyone to generically describe therapeutic salicylic acid. Its value as a trademark was lost. Kleenex®, Xerox®, Google®, and Sheetrock® also face this threat. So what? In my professional opinion, a small entrepreneur should *aspire* to achieve such a risk for his own trademark. If you eventually find a real and present danger that your trademark will become a generic term, then congratulations! Joyously cross that gangplank when you come to it. Thereby are we neatly led to the next lesson in our pirate's professional guide, "the famous trademark."

FOOTNOTE

[1] Be aware that this chapter presents generalities and principles of US law, only. Details, nuances, variances, and exceptions abound. For example, in spite of the general rule that a trademark does not exist until used, your trademark can be essentially "preregistered" on an "Intent to Use" list at the Trademark Office. This list is a legislative creation that largely benefits big business wherein significant "branding" expenses may be accrued long before a product ever reaches the public. The "intent to use" list helps protect that investment.

# 12

# What is a "Famous Trademark," and Why Should I Care?

*Pirate's Rule #12: (The Rule of Gross Tonnage) Big ones run over wee ones, unless wee ones are very wily.*

Once upon a time law was simple, so simple that, "ignorance of the law," was really and truly, "no excuse," for any malefactor. In those days, laws did not change willy-nilly, and the principles were solid as the Rock of Gibraltar. Anybody with a little horse sense could understand them.

Trademark law was that way. Oh, we grant that the good and sensible Common Law of trademark got "sophisticated" by a bunch of arbitrary statutes. But these statutes, by and large, merely implemented what we already knew to be law. Practicing members of the Venerated Guild of Snooty Scalawags Posing as Brilliant Oracles (a.k.a. "lawyers") could dress up common sense with a few ornamental Latin phrases[1] and confidently secure their fees with little fear that their advice might be far from the mark, and with little worry that their pronouncements might not be anchored in sound precedent. In short, all was right with the world.

This, of course, could not be tolerated.

With careful choice of physicians, and enough silver crossing palms, even the best of health can be undone. And so it was with trademark law. In this case, the prescribed quackery was the _Federal Trademark Dilution Act of 1995_. This act[2] departed from established law, and accorded special status to "famous" trademarks. It adventurously sallied forth to abandon tried, true, and lawful concepts, venturing into realms governed by vague, but newly fashionable, ideas like "tarnishing" and "blurring"[3]

Such terminology makes the whole issue sound rather minor. Tarnished, blurred; Nothing that a little polish and a pair of reading specs cannot fix.

But it is not minor.

This is, in fact, a major issue. Up to that time, a trademark was a trademark was a trademark. If one trademark resembled another trademark, then a straightforward test could be applied to determine whether either infringed the other. All lawyers learned it in the first year of law school. We call it the "likelihood of confusion test."[4] Under rule of this test could flourish, for example, a LEXUS automobile and a LEXIS online research system with nary a whimper of litigation. Further, Apple Records® and Apple Computers® could live, if not in peaceful harmony, then at least in grumpy coexistence. This was so because, for anyone capable of distinguishing a small posterior orifice from a hinged arm joint, there was no likelihood of confusion.[5] They were not in the same streams of commerce.

But when our legislators (bless their lobbied little hearts) created the status, "famous marks" this simple and equitable rule got moved to the third class steerage berthing in order to provide preferred seating for a wealthy and privileged few. This new status dictates that if your mark is "famous" you need no longer abide by the "Likelihood of Confusion" rule. Your mark could now be infringed by mere "dilution" or "tarnishment,"…whatever that means.

This jury-rigged statutory rust bucket was sailed out to clear the sea lanes for high tonnage leviathans dubbed "famous." The battle plan was to flank established law and create a situation in which, no matter how disparate their markets, one little trademark could still be found to unlawfully "tarnish" or "dilute" a big famous mark and thereby draw litigious cannon fire. But only the big guys could actually execute this maneuver. Sauce for the goose was no longer sauce for the gander.

On the whole, this arbitrary rearrangement of well settled law was about as popular (with the courts) as a torch juggler in the ammunition magazine. The Supreme Court gunners blasted it out of the water as soon as it got into range.[6]

However, they say a legislature, "once bought should stay bought." So in unswerving loyalty to this particular established tradition, Congress slapped on some hemp and tar (the sailors version of duct tape and chewing gum), jibed violently, and came around for another drunken pass.[7] That is to say, they patched up the statute and launched it *again*, adding language to clearly communicate that they intend to turn established law on its ear.

Thus far the Supreme Court's gunners have not been presented with opportunity for another broadside. So at present this unseaworthy statutory coracle sails as the law of the land.[8] Accordingly, under the present status quo, the great and powerful now get a pass on the old standard under which the rest of the unwashed masses must squeeze themselves for protection.

In thumbnail explanation of the present situation, *if a mark is a "famous mark" then, essentially any use of a mark in any stream of commerce, no matter how remote, that brings to mind any famous mark, may be pronounced an unlawful "dilution" or "tarnishment" of the famous mark's sacred and true meaning.* And further, mere use of something similar may be only one of many roads to this evil end. *Even use of a mark that is utterly quite the opposite from a famous mark may lead to Purgatory or worse.*

What a mess.

Unfortunately, in their attempt to, for the favored few, render moot the "probability of confusion" standard, our legislative bodies have opened a fresh, new, and unpredictable flagon of legless, slimy, subterranean dirt dwellers bearing brand new questions. Lead amongst these lyric-like interrogatories are:

☠ How famous must a mark be, to be "famous"?
and
☠ How can I dilute thee? (Let me count the ways.)

With respect to the first of these questions, it seems everybody now expects or hopes for admission to the "Famous Marks Club."[9] For example, Mensa recently undertook a suit for trademark dilution.  Yes, indeed, that magnificent and universally admired organization......(What is it called again?).... in righteous indignation filed a lawsuit to protect its universally recognized identity.  (What was that name, again?)  Note that this organization (What was their title?) *did prevail* in their suit.[10]  The fact that most people have never heard of them is apparently not a strong indicator of fame, legally speaking.

The simple truth is, nobody knows who the famous club members are.  With respect to answering this question, as cases arise, we appear to be headed for an "I can't tell you what it is, but I know it if I see it," principle of legal discernment.  This does not bode well for clear sailing directions.

With no clear star to steer by, navigation gets tricky.  The key "degree of recognition" standard laid out for guidance in the act appears to provide a circular definition.  "...a mark is famous if it is widely recognized by the general consuming public of the United States."[11]  In other words, it is famous if it is famous.  This, while perhaps true in theory, is not potentially useful information in practice.

Perchance, if the courts continue on the course laid in under the "Mensa" decision, above, ultimate achievement of equity will come from all marks being effectively deemed "famous."  If that happened, then in all cases, "stream of commerce" involved would be moot, as would "likelihood of confusion."  But the playing field would be level.  With the Internet now making world-wide commercial presence available to even the most humble seafarer, automatic entitlement to "famous" status is a not unreasonable expectation.

With respect to the second question, ("How can I dilute thee?") an important matter to note is that mere use of a similar mark is not the only route to litigation.  It seems that one can infringe by being *too* different.  In demonstration of this, a recent case demonstrated that use of a mark diametrically *dissimilar* to another mark can get us into litigious shallows. We refer here, to the case popularly known as *NORTH FACE v. SOUTH BUTT* wherein the former sued the latter for trademark dilution.[12]  It is difficult to imagine two more dissimilar marks.

What does all this mean to the aspiring entrepreneur, or his legal counsel?  Well, first, it means that **trademark choice instantly became more risky.  And trademark searches just became more complex, expensive, and less dependable**.

Before settling on a new trademark, not only should a competent "likelihood of confusion" infringement search be executed, but also a dilution search.  In doing this search, we must remember that we don't really know what dilution may comprise. Ideally, a dilution search should address not only similar marks, but also dissimilar marks that call to mind contrast with some other mark, as in South Butt and North Face, above.  Watch out also for "parody" marks that specifically set out to parody other marks.  (We wish you good luck with that one, but don't hold a lot of hope for success.)

For sure, a business owner should be advised to take even greater care than has been traditional in choosing a new trademark. The cost of a bad choice can be economically disastrous to a large business, and fatal to a small one.

%%%%%%%%%%%%%%%%%%%%%%%%%%%%%%%%%%%%%%%%
FOOTNOTES
[1] Quid latine dictum sit, altum videtur.  ("Anything said in Latin sounds impressive.")

[2] Apparently based on previously unknown definitions for terms such as "fairness", "justice", and "equality."

[3] The "blurring" concept concisely demonstrating that justice, though not really blind, may, indeed, need eyeglasses.

[4] *Polaroid Corp. v. Polaroid Elect. Corp.*, 287 F.2d 492 (2d Cir.), cert. denied, 368 US 820 (1961).

[5] There were states, like California, congenitally obsessed with privileges of the rich and famous (See California's anti-paparazzi law codified at Cal. Civ. Code § 1708.8.) that had ventured away from our solidly founded trademark principles. But California is, after all.....California. (See California Business and Professions Code Sections 14330-14335, Article 12. Dilution.)*

*(OK, so we do grudgingly concede that Tennessee has a dilution statute, too. But hardly anybody uses it. See Tenn. Code Ann. 47-26-513(a). Also see *AutoZone, Inc v. Tandy Corp.* 373 F. 3d 786, 801, 6th Cir. 2004, "There are no Tennessee cases that analyze this statute...")

[6] *Moseley v. V Secret Catalogue, Inc.*, 537 US 418 (2003). In this case, deigning to address the issue of "dilution" only, the court declined to explore the question of whether anything could possibly "tarnish" the name and reputation of Victoria's Secret.

[7] *Trademark Dilution Revision Act of 2006*

[8] See footnote 7, supra. After a majority of justices left the Dilution Act holed and grounded, Congress (bless their lobbied little hearts) composed a snappy and well-defended legislative reply to the Supreme Court decision. Their carefully composed Congressional reply was essentially, "Oh, yeah?" Tommy Smothers would have been proud. Quoting their revised act in greater detail, the owner of a famous mark can prevail against another person who, *"at any time after the owner's mark has become famous, commences use of a*

*mark or trade name in commerce as a designation of source that is likely to cause dilution by blurring or dilution by tarnishment of the famous mark, regardless of the presence or absence of actual or likely confusion, of competition, or of actual economic injury."* 15 USC. § 1125(c)(1) (2006)

[9] *Not* inclusive of Groucho, Harpo, Chico, Zeppo, Gummo, or Karl.

[10] They settled. *American Mensa, Ltd. v. Inpharmatica, Ltd. et al.,* No. 07-3283 (D. Md filed Dec. 6, 2007). Apparently, the fact that my spell checker does not recognize "Mensa" is not a strong indicator in determining fame either.

[11] Referring to the act of footnote 8, supra, Sec 2 (c) (2) (i)-(iii), the question of whether a mark is "Famous" depends upon,
☠     The duration, extent, and geographic reach of advertising and publicity of the mark, whether advertised or publicized by the owner or third parties.
☠     The amount, volume, and geographic extent of sales of goods or services offered under the mark.
☠     The extent of actual recognition of the mark.
☠     Whether the mark was registered under the Act of March 3, 1881, or the Act of February 20, 1905, or on the principal register.

[12] *United States District Court for the Eastern District of Missouri, Eastern Div, The North Face Apparel Corp., v. Williams Pharmacy, Inc., et al., Case No. 09-CV-02029 , Plaintiff's Pre-hearing memorandum of Law, in Support of its Motion for a Preliminary Injunction.* A dispute in which the defendant is reputed to have succinctly pointed out that, (essentially) anyone who cannot

distinguish "face" from "butt" has more pressing issues than trademark confusion.

*This chapter adapted with permission of the* Nashville Bar Journal *from an article of the same name, and by the same author. Their kind authorization is gratefully acknowledged.*

# 13

# *Copyrights*

## *Pirate's Rule #13: Dead men have no best interests.*

Legally and statutorily speaking, copyrights bestow upon their owners a rather vague and messy list of privileges over their works. These privileges include rights to prevent others from reproducing, selling, adapting, performing or displaying the work of the copyright owner. This is simple to say, but there be devils stalkin' in the details. In application, they can become a touch difficult to nail down.

Copyrights exist to prevent, quite specifically, protected works from being *copied*. Copying means *only actual copying*. This is in contrast to patents and trademarks that prohibit close similarity no matter how the similarity is achieved. Not so in the case of copyrights.

Copyrights do not protect against production or sale of virtually identical musical works, sculptures, or pictures, etc., by different composers or artists. So if, for example, someone else independently produces a work that strongly resembles your own then it may be suspicious but it is of itself neither a crime nor infringement. Mere similarity is, of itself alone, insufficient to comprise infringement. If a similar piece is not the result of an outright *copy*, then it does not infringe.

Further, copyrights do not protect inventions. Copyrights do not protect trademarks. Copyrights do not protect mere titles. Copyrights do not protect mere ideas. These are, with some intriguing exceptions, guiding stars of copyright law and principles.[1] (See Appendix II, Tactical Matrix.)

However, a quick gander at the constant flow of directionless court cases drifting daily into our law books will tend to shake your confidence in these guide stars. The problem is not with the navigator's stars, though. The problem is the distracting cargo. Even King Neptune himself cannot predict the seaworthiness of any given case, assuming enough gold ballast gets loaded aboard. (Well, that is except to predict that the sea lawyers will turn a nice profit.)

But addressing first things first, our new recruits should be more interested in practical issues of how one actually acquires copyright protection. The good news is that theoretically and legally speaking, as soon as a new work is created, it acquires copyright protection. This is true before the first hint of registration is begun. The bad news is that in practical application no US copyright can actually be defended unless it is registered.

Fortunately, US copyright registration is a reasonably simple process. But it is also relatively easy to screw up. If you undertake your own copyright registrations, and you do screw it up, you likely will not be made aware of your errors until you need to defend the copyright. This is the worst time for it to happen. Do not invite such an outcome.

My point here is that if your work is worth protecting, it is worth protecting correctly and effectively. Properly executed US Copyrights are not expensive, at least not compared to other forms of IP protection. If you want one done right, hire an attorney who knows the subject, and get it done correctly the first time.

## *Termination Rights*

Copyright transfers, assignments, licenses, conveyances, etc., are the means by which an author or artist gets paid by assigning to somebody else possession or use of his copyright. However, copyright statutes include provisions for eventual termination and reversion of these rights for anybody other than the original owner or heirs. This is popularly called, "a second bite of the apple" for the original owner.

The way things have evolved, copyright assignment agreements often contractually run for entire lifetimes and more. So, to rebalance this situation, our legislators created assignment termination provisions. These statutes *purport to dictate that every copyright assignment revert to its original owner's estate after passage of a fixed, but very large, number of years, no matter what any contract says.* But, this fixed number of years is so large that the original owner is unlikely to enjoy much benefit from it. (See Pirate's Rule #13: "Dead men have no best interests.")

Further, the statutes erect a maze of obstacles between the original author or composer and the benefits they purport to offer. Navigation through these termination minefields is excruciatingly complex and fraught with danger. If you have assigned your copyrights, engage a copyright attorney now, now, now, to plot a course to future freedom. If you want to exercise your rights under these statutes, there are actions that you *must* execute at fixed points *in advance*. Miss the time window, and your rights are forfeit.

This morass appears to have been created to further the interests of the middlemen who are loath to surrender the fruits of other men's labors and talents. Although dead authors and artists indeed have no best interests, the middlemen who buy up the rights to their creations do. So, although the statutes were created under the guise of benefitting artists, the real recipients of its largess are publishers and other middlemen. Experience has proved this to be true.

That said, however, many members of the artistic community originally promoted adoption of this statutory mess with righteous fervor. Apparently they subscribed to the philosophy of riverboat gambler Canada Bill Jones, "...*it's crooked, but it's the only game in town.*" Now they are learning the extent of their foolishness. We hope that you, shipmate, will learn from their mistakes. The following instructions may assist in this.

## *Best Practices to Retain Copyright Profitability*

If you want to preserve your intellectual property rights for yourself and your progeny, as opposed to making a gift of your long term rights to parasitic middlemen (who are quietly becoming unnecessary anyway) modern technologies make the following measures feasible and preferable.

☠ Always put a dated © copyright notice on your works. Identify the author, composer, or owner. This helps to preserve rights to the fullest, and anyway, it is simple good manners to give potential infringers fair warning. A dog ought to bark before it bites.

☠Register your copyright before your publish.  Do not release your copyright ownership and rights.

☠Retain personal control of your publishing and distribution. With modern technology, this is cheap and easy.  Alternatively, engage someone to assist you under contract.  But, in any case, remain the official publisher yourself.

☠If you do sell your rights, get a big (and I do mean large) nonrefundable price paid in full, up front.  Otherwise, do not sell them.  If you do not get a major fee up front, you may not receive any fee at all.  So, get the cash in hand, first.  Collect and stow your treasure ashore, so to speak, before you set sail in what may prove a leaky business deal.

## How to Become a Famous Dead Artist

Over the passage of several decades this poor brigand has witnessed emerging fame of more than one deceased or soon-to-be deceased artist who exhibited what we adjudged dubious talent. Yours truly at first agonized over what appeared to be his personal lack of artistic discernment.  He clearly could not even identify what was worth stealing.

But eventually he was relieved to have his pirate's eyes and instincts strike upon a pattern common to many achieving such late renown.  The problem was not that he could not detect beauty.  The problem was that he failed to recognize the brilliant piracies executed right before our eyes, and the wool pulled over them, in the "art world."  This was a most astounding revelation.  So here for your exploitation and entertainment do we offer the benefit of this discerning artistic insight, pirate style.

The approach comprises seven steps.  Variations are feasible, but these seven steps most clearly communicate the spirit of the method. We would wish ye to use this plan in good health, but that would rather contradict yer purposes. Use it to become dead famous.

Step 1: Create and preserve a large body of intuitively identifiable and potentially transportable work.[2] Quality is not important. "Recognizability" is the key. To develop a genuine distinguishing style is commendable but not necessary. Mere consistently recognizable incompetence is quite sufficient to meet the artistic standard required. Keep a collection of your creations in an easily accessible group.

Step 2: Develop a unique and compelling background story upon which to capitalize. Your tale needs a strong theme that will generate sympathy. If you manage to plausibly cast yourself as a downtrodden, disadvantaged, poverty-stricken, terminally ill war victim and man-of-the-people, you're in. The yarn absolutely must include a limited expectation of continued personal survival. Presence of this short life expectancy has important strategic ramifications, as will become clear below. If you cannot immediately draw on advanced age to fulfill this requirement, then illness or notorious drug/alcohol abuse should suffice. In assembling your woeful narrative, fabrication is almost always superior to truth, so apply your best talents. However if your sad story is actually true, it is OK to use it anyway.

Step 3: Make your body of works, and your sad story, known to a select few collectors, museums, publishers, or other promoters. Seed a few examples of your work around where they are likely to be noticed.

Step 4: Once your works and story are known to these collectors, museums, publishers, or other promoters, make it known that you are altruistically anxious to sign over, for a pittance, rights to a major portion of your work.

Step 5: Close the deal with your buyer. If you have sown your seeds with the right scoundrels, you should find at least one who will agree to accept your deal, but purportedly, "only in the greater public interest," of course, while quietly calculating his potential personal profits.

Step 6: Optionally, live just long enough to appear in a significant number of art shows, book signings, magazine reviews, or TV/radio interviews to promote your work for the buyer. (Expect to be pleasantly transported, wined, dined, and lodged in the process.)

Step 7: Expire, or at least accomplish a reasonable facsimile thereof. To fake your own disappearance at sea might be sufficient, but weigh the pros and cons of this carefully. Should the wrong persons find you insufficiently dead, they might helpfully orchestrate your more permanent demise to protect their financial interests.

The intended result of all this is to give prospective collectors, dealers or other purchasers inexpensive first dibs on your large, but finite and discontinued body of work. The plan is to leave these potential investors plenty of opportunity to "discover" and extol the genius of your late artistic talent, the products of which you have made conveniently available for commercial exploitation. They can accordingly sing your praises in expectation of generating a tidy personal profit for themselves by:

☠ smoothly unloading your works on unsuspecting art-snob suckers at great profit,

*and/or,*

☠ borrowing money against your art as collateral,

*and/or,*

☠ donating pieces to museums or public institutions thereby creating millions of dollars in charitable tax deductions for themselves.

They can do all this while appearing to discover and selflessly rescue a previously unnoticed but deserving talent (you). What a deal!

In advance preparation, to maximize future return, a team of conspirators could publically trade your art back and forth amongst themselves, jacking up the price on each sale, until it appraises at levels undreamt by less sophisticated cut-throats. (Search the Web for the term "Whitewater" to get details on how to execute this part of the scheme. It appears to have been perfected as a means of real estate scam.) Your plan is to get potential promoters to recognize this opportunity and find it difficult to resist.

Voila! (Sorry I should say, "Blimey!") You have made your creations an inviting investment with promise of large potential profits. This provides motivation for collectors or dealers to proclaim the inestimable value of your creations in order to realize these profits. Thereby, you establish fame for yourself and fortunes for piratical bamboozlers who use your art to exploit overfunded but under-informed bamboozlees[3].

Do not feel badly about this, for as that previously quoted pillar of moral authority, Canada Bill Jones teaches us, *"It is a sin to let a sucker keep his money."* The suckers who buy into your legacy will probably be grateful for the prestigious privilege of giving up a portion of theirs to do so.

You certainly will not be the first to follow this circuitous course to fame. But you may be the first to actively plan the route for yourself in advance. Understand you will not personally gain much tangible benefit, for under this plan you are, or had better soon be, dead. Dead men have no best interests. And your heirs are unlikely to benefit, for you've already sold off the property (well, except for potential termination rights previously discussed). Middlemen are the monetary winners. But, butter me backside and call me a sea biscuit, you got famous. You may expect your story to eventually, become the subject of glowing biographies and doctoral dissertations.

Mission accomplished.

%%%%%%%%%%%%%%%%%%%%%%%%%%%%%%%%%%%%%%%%%

FOOTNOTES

[1] Interesting tidbit: In divergence from what one might expect in view of these principles, copyright is not used to protect typeface. Typeface, due to its technological history, falls under design patents. In apparently continuing contradiction, copyrights, not patents, *are* used to protect ship hull designs. Trust a sailor to wring out the cheapest, longest-term protection for his own privileges.

[2] Paintings are good. Immobile wall graffiti seems, prima facie, a poor choice. Statuettes would fill the bill. Ten ton stone sculptures probably are not well adapted to your purpose. Music and poetry should serve acceptably.

[3] *Bamboozlee: Mark, dupe, sap, sucker, gull, chump, mug, patsy, easy target, pushover, fall guy, soft touch, dumb money, cooperative* <u>*victim*</u>.

# 14

# Protection of Software

# and

# "Business Methods"

*Pirate's Rule #14: There be demons in protecting software!*

Nobody really knows how to protect software. In an attempt to overcome such deficiency the US recognized "Business Method Patents" that permit patents on software. This produced indifferent success and much litigation. Most of the rest of the world considers software inventions unpatentable. China is working out a protection method based on a special copyright regime. But copyright tends to be so narrow that little more hope rests there.

As the situation presently stands, no single means of software protection is likely to be sufficient. So for software protection, I generally recommend a tactic known as sea as "concentration of fire," bringing every applicable legal or business tool and weapon to bear, concurrently, and in coordination, all with the same target in their sights. Where one weapon is momentarily less effective, another may pound it harder. Concentrated combinations may yet carry the day to protect your software.

Another tactic, popular with big corporate players, is to amass and exploit sheer volume in software IP ownership. It appears that software behemoths, Microsoft®, for instance, buy up thousands of software patents as a defensive tactic. The philosophy is that if they own enough patents, they should be able to identify or combine enough of them to get around other patents that might otherwise prove obstructive to them. Failing that, they can always use their vast portfolio of patents to countersue any accuser.[2]

The software market was once confined almost exclusively to these leviathans. But nowadays, it has, like the music industry, come within reach of the common man. (The plethora of iPhone® software applications, are an example) However, for small and large alike, at the present excruciatingly slow rate of examination for business method patents, you can expect that any software will be obsolete long before the patent for it issues. So the main value of your software patent may rest in its value as a defense against infringement accusations.

By all means, consider applying for patents on your software. Register copyrights for your software code and screen graphics. For the screen graphics, also register trademarks where appropriate. Additionally, consider the possibility of maintaining trade secret status, particularly if specific hardware is an integral component of your overall system. Protect, and consider dividing, your source code before copyright registration. The US Copyright Office Website, at last inspection, offered some good tips on preservation of trade secrets in the copyright regime.

Adhere closely to the previously discussed three part anti-pirate tactic of:

- ☠ Product; Honest
- ☠ Price; Fair
- ☠ Demand; Met

And, pay close attention to yer fickle business and market winds, mate. In the software and media world, they changes sudden-like. So be ready to reset yer sails accordingly and quickly.

%%%%%%%%%%%%%%%%%%%%%%%%%%%%%%%%%%%%%%%%

FOOTNOTES

[1] In illustration, the Wall Street Journal (Friday, 2 September 2011) relates that Nokia® recently sold approximately 2,000 patents to Mosaid Technologies, Inc., while still retaining an arsenal of 30,000 other patents. With this purchase, Mosaid®, which produces no products at all, holds a total of about 5,400 patents it exploits to undertake royalty or licensing demands, litigations, or settlements.

[2] The end result of suits tends to be "cross licensing." In a cross license, we agree that *you* can use certain selections of *my* patented technology, in exchange for which I can use certain selections of *your* patented technology. Then, we all go home grumpy, except for the lawyers, who get paid handsomely, no matter what the outcome.

# 15

# Recording Artists Don't Need No Stinkin' Middlemen!

1

*Pirate's Rule #15: Recording artists do not get rich through recording contracts. Scurvy middlemen do.*

Recording artists make their real money on the road as performing artists. This rule holds true even for artists who go gold or platinum.

As with every rule, there are, I suppose, exceptions. But those few recording artists who actually generate significant income *for themselves* seldom do it in the recording studio. For the recording artists under recording contracts, the dice are generally loaded and the deck stacked against them. A cursory review of recording contracts tendered over the last several years confirms their generally usurious character.

In truth, the recording artist in the studio has historically earned far more revenue for the middlemen than for himself (or herself). The way an artist generated real income was by going on concert tour. It's the concerts that built up the artist's bank account. To be concise, the recording studio made the artist famous, and concert tours paid the artist's bills.[2]

So although recordings sales were the source of revenue for the recording labels, they were for the artist, merely a means of advertising. Now, understanding this, ya' gotta' ask yourself one question, "Which is better, *selling* your advertisements, or *giving them away for free?*" The answer is rather obvious. If you want your advertisements to get wide distribution, you don't demand that people pay for them. You give them away.

But until the digital revolution, the middlemen (record labels) held all the cards. The middlemen decided who got recorded, what got recorded, what got distributed, and for what price. The middlemen decided how much got paid and to whom. And they bloomin' sure were not giving anything away. The middlemen had a solid lock on the industry because they controlled the technology. But now, all that has changed. The artist no longer needs the middlemen...Well, at least not *those* middlemen.

The artist can have his own recording studio for a pittance. He can be his own producer. He can distribute his products directly online. The artist can become famous without signing a single recording contract, and can become financially successful by corralling that fame into successful concert tours. T'ain't mere theory. This is demonstrated fact.[3]

He don't need no stinkin' middlemen.

In response to this new paradigm, a number of Web based ventures have sprung up to assist the aspiring, self-producing, artist, and help put the artist in contact with potential fans. A quick Web search will turn up quite a passel. Lift your eye patch and give them a look-see.

%%%%%%%%%%%%%%%%%%%%%%%%%%%%%%%%%%%%%%%

FOOTNOTES

[1] Approximate translation: "No stinkin' middlemen." Literal translation, "Prohibited, middle person bad smell."

[2] Today, however, the recording studios standardize contracts to additionally tap into the artist's concert profits and other non-record income. They want a cut of *everything*, apparently hoping to prove that artists will sign *anything*. Watch your manager or agent closely if he presents one of these "360 [degree]" or "all asset" or "multiple rights" contracts. Confirm that he is getting his cut from the same side and portion of the pie that feeds you, too. If he is not, then that weasel has likely slipped his cable, and may be secretly sailing under his own Jolly Roger. Pirates are everywhere.

[3] As an example of this, we offer the self-defined indy/pop/rock band *Bare Naked Ladies*. For those who do not recognize the name, check'em out. They are consummate musical

artists.  *Bare Naked Ladies* distinguished themselves as (fully clothed) pioneers, making their music available online and, in due course, *selling out* their first tour without ever having signed with a record label.*

Being admirably perceptive, the Beatles® are another example of smart performers who caught onto the economic disparity between performers and middlemen, early.  They countered the situation by creating *their own* record label, Apple Records®. That way, they could get rich from both concerts *and* recordings.

The darlin' favorites of my own heart are Perpetuam Jazille®, (a rising um...pop group...sort of) from Slovenia.  Yep, Slovenia. This bonny crew from a small, young country has booked concerts world-wide...without assistance of a label.  Their Web videos have gone viral.  Apparently, in the music business, not only the middlemen are obsolete.  It seems location is also no longer a factor, so New York and Los Angeles had best look for a way to retire from their position in the van of the battle formation, gracefully.

*http://www.myspace.com/barenakedladies
(*They're Canadian, aye?*)

# 16

# What's the Big Deal?

## (Bootleg File Sharing)

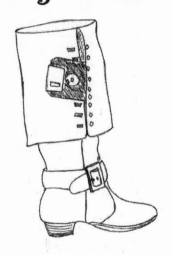

## Pirate's Rule #16: Pirates exploit unenforceable laws.

Pirates exploit unenforceable laws. So do not trust unenforceable laws to protect your interests. This chapter addresses bootleg file sharing, and is mostly aimed at other sea lawyers. But, it's OK to read over their shoulders. Originally published years ago, *it was received in a most hostile and dismissive manner by them what previously comprised the late, great, recording industry. Yet, its predictions have emerged as reality. So figger it's worth the readin'. (That's me way of givin' a saltwater toffee-nosed, "I told 'em so." Meb'be them "shining wits"[1] will recognize the magnificent genius of me prophesies, next time, if they manage to survive long enough to experience a "next time.")*

When 'Omer smote 'is bloomin' lyre,
He'd 'eard men sing by land an' sea
And what 'e thought he might require,
'E went and took - the same as me.

The market girls and fishermen,
The shepherds an' the sailors, too,
They 'eard old songs turn up again,
But kept it quiet – same as you!

They knew 'e stole; 'e knew they knowed.
They didn't tell, nor make a fuss,
But winked at 'Omer down the road,
An' 'e winked back - the same as us![2]

This short ditty above was penned by Rudyard Kipling a century, or so ago. His point was (and if anyone had the right to say it, he did) that music and poetry inevitably belong to *all* of us. *Inevitably.* So there's no use getting your knickers in a knot about it.

It is no big deal.

This is a particularly relevant issue, today, for, in the recording industry, this matter *is* a big deal. We have the nicely lobbied Digital Millennium Copyright Act to prove it.

However, "What's the big deal?" is the question most often thrown in our faces by freebooting Internet music down loaders.

Most of us do not care to admit that they ask a valid question. Our response has become a standardized recitation, easily mouthed without exercising a single brain cell. "Downloading or file sharing is stealing," we say. "Downloading or file sharing is theft, just like shoplifting." The purported electronic burglars stare at us blankly, as if that response makes no sense.

They stare at us because our answer is not true, and *they know it*. They know that we self-righteous intellectual property defenders are on tenuous ground and incapable of defending our position beyond rhetorical arm waving. The fact that they know it says much in their favor. It indicates that the questioners have managed to preserve and protect a fair amount of moral perspective and objective reason from the ravages of arbitrary statute and institutional propaganda. (How's that for an inflammatory mouthful?)

We can, and must, learn from them. To deal with legal concepts of intellectual property, we legal practitioners (read "conformists") have necessarily learned to disregard instinctive, common sense understanding of what property is and how one may own it. But our narrow and skewed legalistic approach to understanding this is no longer sufficient.

Now, we of "the establishment" must absorb a bigger picture. We must regain the unsullied perspective of those who question our "lawful" contentions. If we fail to do so we risk being overtaken by obsolescence.

Available technology now demands that we reacquire a morally and logically defensible understanding of intellectual property. We must, as do the so called "pirates," look beyond simple statute. This is because we no longer have the upper hand, *and they know it*. We must *un*learn our fantasies of law and recognize them for what they are, mere statutes backed by nothing more than limited (and failing) powers of coercion. We must re-broaden our focus and relearn what we, otherwise, would perceive instinctively.

So what is it that we should, as mentioned, perceive instinctively about property? Well, first, we need to understand as a child, for even every child understands the term, "mine." What is mine is not yours. My toy schooner is *my* toy schooner. You may have a toy schooner just like mine, but mine is still mine. The fact that you might possess, or even fabricate, a toy like mine is irrelevant to my own possession of my own toy. My property is still wholly mine and I have no cause for complaint against you for having or making one like it. No fundamental wrong is perpetuated by the copy of my toy.

With the exception of common Trademark law[3], this is in complete contradiction of intellectual property legal principles. Those of us (primarily youths) who have not yet had their instincts dulled or perverted by institutionalized propaganda instantly recognize this. Those of us who have not subjugated their moral instincts to smug authoritative decrees look quizzical when told that downloading is theft.

This is because music downloading may be statutorily illegal. But...and get this very clear...*it certainly is not, "stealing" or "theft"*...at least not in the way that we morally or legally understand the terms.[4]

Again, this is elementary.

If I take your music CD, that is theft. Now, I have it and you do not. You are deprived of your property in order that I might possess it. (Lawyers call this "conversion.") But if you merely copy it for me, then we both have one. Nobody was deprived of his music. That is common sense. Only by artificial statutory dictate (copyright statutes) does the copy become illegal. (It feels silly to need to explain this. But not understanding it makes us look even *more* silly.)

To people who still possess moral sense, arbitrary statutes have little moral authority. Only so long as statutes are perceived as reasonable will compliance be likely, or even recognized as imposing any sort of obligation.

Thus, when music downloading appears merely *malum prohibitum*, compliance becomes less obligatory. That is a fact of simple, unadulterated reality, unsullied by arbitrary establishment rules-based fantasy. (*Malum prohibitum* means, loosely, "merely prohibited because some self-interested dweeb managed to get a rule enacted.")

To put it another way, for those with moral sense, the moral chink in our armor of intellectual property rules is easy to identify. The chink is this; "property" is something that only one of us can wholly possess at any instant in time. "Copies" are not "thefts."

However, our rules of intellectual property deny this. They decree treat replication to be wrongful. This does not make the rules evil. It merely makes them arbitrary.

We know this, or should know this, by instinct and common sense. Those of us (primarily youth) who have not had our moral sense dulled by mass obedience training instantly recognize it. Common sense is all it takes to recognize that there are no natural or inherent property rights to music, or poetry, or images. If this were not so, the law could not morally place universal limits on the periods of time during which ownership is permitted.

The not-yet-bended possessors of common moral sense know that when we copy music, we simply create more music to share. They know that, copyrights notwithstanding, copies deprive no one of his music.

Furthermore, him what comes seekin' justice best not come sticky-fingered.[5] The recording industry, however, is perceived to have less than pristine digits.  At this point in technological and economic history, paying fifteen or twenty dollars for a music CD marketed at teenagers is largely considered *un*fair.  At fifteen to twenty dollars, it makes you wonder if the sellers are not, in reality, the biggest monopolistic pirates on the high seas.  Facing such a marketing price gouging combination, the availability of do-it-yourself replication using cheap, easy technology looks increasingly attractive and more rational.  Supposed "moral authority" becomes a big washout.

Purported moral authority, being, in the view of the copier, reduced to the point of irrelevance, this leaves only force of reason or coercive power to shore up the system.

Cleaving to force of reason, we argue that that creativity is stifled by those who bypass the copyright system.  But, this argument comes across as ludicrous.  Only the industrial establishment is being stifled, and to many consumers, that seems a *good* thing.  Anyway, home production technology is fast rendering the large recording industry irrelevant as a source of creative motivation just as the Internet is rendering it irrelevant as a source of distribution.  This makes quick work of "reason" as a bulwark to encourage statutory compliance.

Having surrendered both moral authority and force of reason as grounds for conforming to the rules, we are left to depend only upon coercion to protect the fat of the recording industry.  This explains the explosion of summonses and lawsuits for copyright infringement.

These legal actions, however, have the unmistakable of scent of the dead about them.  They resemble the twitches of a body already sunk beyond any hope of resuscitation, for such coercive, punitive methods are inevitably doomed to failure.  A few scoundrels might slither a couple of suits through, but only until the courts recognize the wasteful multiplication of their resulting workload, and put a kibosh on such projects. The federal courts simply cannot handle such volume as would be demanded by the potential numbers of frivolous anti-downloading lawsuits.

Furthermore, few such suits can be expected to recover enough to finance themselves. Most freebooting downloaders are, we might expect, inherently judgment proof, for they have few or no assets. Ultimately, a proliferation of such suits will merely render potential customers irretrievably hostile. So fades coercion as a tool.

With little or no moral authority, force of reason or coercive power, the battle is clearly lost. The only commercially viable approach for the recording industry is to surrender to reality. Statutes be damned, the fat feeders must slim down or they will be left to starve. The industry must stop attacking its primary source of clientele and, instead, develop new business models that make statutory compliance an economically reasonable option. Recent Internet business models providing cut-price online downloads are an excellent example of such a model. (The members of legal profession can help them understand and achieve this.)

These are elements of a cycle that repeats again and again.[6] Take the printing press as an example. Printing presses and digital technology are children of the same mother. They are information media.

Printing presses gave the world cheap, widely available access to recorded matter previously controlled by a select few gatekeepers. When William Tyndale, for one, set out to maximize the wonderful new printing technologies and liberate the information they could reproduce, he so upset the previous gatekeepers that they burned him at the stake.[7] But, ultimately, there simply were not enough bonfires and stakes to go around. The gatekeepers were trying to contain a flood with a picket fence. It was hopeless.

Tyndale's story bears a strong resemblance to our present situation. In today's world, our gatekeepers are in the recording industry. Just as the gatekeepers did in Tyndale's day, they are trying to effect mass obedience through coercion. Just as in Tyndale's day, they will fail.

The gatekeepers must adjust to accommodate the new technological and economic paradigm. In Tyndale's day, books became easily reproduced. Prices and availability had to adjust accordingly. As a result, today, books are literally tens of thousands of times cheaper than they were when the printing press was first invented.

Now, the electronic recording industry is faced with the same situation. Widely available technology demands that they revise their standards of reasonable price and distribution as it did in the time of Tyndale.

The heyday of the fifteen dollar CD is past. The day of forcing a customer to buy 10 songs he does not want just to get a copy of one hit is ended. Cheap recording and reproduction technology are wresting music from the behemoth of industry and handing it back to the masses from whence it came. The production and dissemination of music is returning to its natural place in the homes and on the streets.

We of the legal profession, have an obligation to help our clients, particularly in the entertainment industry, understand these facts because *it is in their best interest to do so.* They call us "counselors." We need to give counsel, now. We need to counsel our clients that in the world of information technology (which includes the recording industry) they face an inevitable cycle.

Those who would survive must learn to ride the cycle, lest they be run over by it. This, too, is an old, old story. It should be no surprise. But each generation must deal with it. Our rules of intellectual property are for using, not abusing. When they are abused, the entire structure eventually collapses.

As mentioned above, paranoid abusive protectionism for so called intellectual property a century ago was apparently the inspiration for Rudyard Kipling when he declaimed, *When 'Omer Smote 'Is Bloomin' Lyre.* All he was saying is, "This is reality. Learn to live with it. Learn to work within it. It's no big deal."

%%%%%%%%%%%%%%%%%%%%%%%%%%%%%%%%%%

FOOTNOTES

[1] Not a Spoonerism.

[2] Kipling, Rudyard, *When 'Omer Smote His Bloomin' Lyre*, Introduction to Barrack-Room Ballads in, <u>The Seven Seas</u>. Publisher: New York : D. Appleton and Co., 1896, [1898]

[3] There is, of course, only one true ancient and common law form of intellectual property, and that is the trademark. (In this we also encompass service mark, trade name, and trade dress.) A trademark is one's good name, and as such, may be owned by only one person at a time. Shakespeare summed this up nicely through his character Iago in *Othello,* "He who steals my purse steals trash...but he who filches from me my good name...doth make me poor, indeed."

[4] "Stealing" and "theft" are broad terms in our vernacular. One can "steal" a jewel, a song, or a kiss, but the understood meaning of the word is different in each case. We can confirm the legal definition of "theft" by a quick reference to *Black's Law Dictionary,* but I, for one, would feel silly citing a reference to support mere common sense.

[5] "He who comes into equity must come with clean hands." (Ancient rule of Common Law syllogism to pirate's rule, "Them what lives in glass houseboats should studiously avoid slingin' shot.")

[6] This cycle can be tracked in a broader context throughout all areas of IP, and particularly in our statute law. The Digital Millennium Copyright Act, hardly a paragon of equity, is one characteristic instance.

[7] Tyndale's outrageous offense, one may recall, for which he was burned at the stake in 1536, was to print unauthorized copies of the Bible.

# 17
# Understanding the Dragon
## IP from the Chinese Perspective

Pirate's Rule #17: The panda is
really a dragon in disguise.
(With contributions by Tracy Kane, Esq.)

100

As fittingly represented by both a dragon and a panda,[1] the People's Republic of China is generally regarded as enigmatic. If this were not so we would not be bombarded regularly by a plethora of abstruse scribbles from every scholar, politico, and two bit social commentator, dashed off in attempt to unwind its mysterious complexities.

In this particular case, however, your humble author aims to present a rather concise and disarmingly simple approach to understanding the intellectual property policies of China. By the end of this chapter, you too will be able to decipher the intent of any IP policy in China (even without reading Mandarin). The method has two steps:

I.  Read the intellectual property provisions of the United States Constitution (Article 1, Section 8, Paragraph 8, as quoted below).

II. Interpret Chinese policy as if this portion of the US Constitution were incorporated into Chinese law.

This may sound crazy, but hear me out. The United States Constitution, Article 1, Section 8, Clause 8 simply specifies that, in order to encourage advancement in knowledge and technology, specifically "science and the useful arts", "authors" and "inventors" will receive a temporary monopoly over their writings and discoveries.[2] In other words, people who create advancements in knowledge and technology get a sole but temporary right to use their advancements now, in exchange for giving the rest of us free use of their advancements later.[3]

This self-same little section of our own constitution also essentially expresses present Chinese policy concerning intellectual property. So, to understand Chinese policy with respect to any IP issue, ask yourself, "Is this a matter that can advance China in technology and knowledge?" If so then consider how China might best exploit it, for that is naturally what China (or anyone else who actually thinks about it in a logical and well informed manner) will do.[4] If it is *not* a matter that can advance China in technology and knowledge, then you can figure that it does not matter much to China, either way. It is a *non*issue, or at least a noneconomic issue, about which China needs not trouble herself. Pop music, films, and other pastimes fall in this latter category.

A caveat; All of this, of course, presupposes that the subject intellectual property is not perceived to "rock the political boat." Rocking the boat is not good and will not be tolerated. Consequently, in a bit of skewed logic, works, for example, that get flagged by the censors (otherwise known as the Great Fire Wall of China overseen by the Ministry of Culture) will not get, or will lose, copyright protection.

Now to fill in some of the details of intellectual property policy in China; Chinese policy is or at least, so far, has been consistently pragmatic, and two pronged. These prongs are:

-Economic advancement ("What is best for China?")
-Political control ("What is best for the Party?")

Though it may not be philosophically acknowledged by "the Party," these two prongs tend to conflict and increasingly so.[5] The desire for advancement and progress can conflict with the desire for political control.

The Chinese government recognizes, to a degree, the cultural contributions of the fine arts. But the Chinese also recognize that significant macroeconomic advancement, on which the Chinese presently seem to have a laser beam focus, comes from science and technology. So the economic interests of China, at least in the near term, are advanced by protecting, hoarding, and exploiting what they have of these technological assets, while acquiring more from the outside.

Political control, on the other hand, is understood to be preserved by limiting, or at least controlling, the importation and flow of information or ideas. For any existing power structure, the introduction of new ideas and attitudes is risky business. Unfettered importation of commentary, literature, music and other products of expression may be viewed as, at best, a mixed blessing, and at worst, as subversive, having tendency to dilute the indigenous culture and destabilize the ship of state while contributing little in the way of concrete and measurable economic advancement.

This lack of significant direct macroeconomic impact is of particular note when trying to understand how the same underlying principles can lead to vastly different policy results. For example, we Americans exist under constant bombardment of entertainment hype and generally seem to possess no appreciation of how little public or macroeconomic impact even the most lucrative of the fine arts have in comparison to most any other commercial endeavor.

This constant barrage of entertainment based publicity can rather skew our perceptions. As a result, we may overestimate the economic value of entertainment by huge proportions particularly when compared to other industries.[6] The Chinese government, by contrast, does not view media and ideas or artistic expression as a "market" per se. In their view, any economic value is outweighed by the potential social harm they may cause if left unsupervised.

This perspective certainly has its benefits for the controlling political party, but it also has its roots in Confucianism, which is an ethical philosophy that is seeing a resurgence in China right now.[7] Consistent with this viewpoint, China makes no attempt to seriously protect its own media or fine arts products from uncontrolled replication. As a result, Chinese film, TV, books, magazines, music, visual arts and the rest are routinely "light-fingered"[8] and the associated businesses and artists are largely left undeveloped and in poverty. At least that is what the artists assert. The Chinese clearly do not see these types of creative endeavors as pure intellectual property the way that patents, trademarks, and trade secrets are. So they receive a wholly different treatment.

China has worked diligently since the passage of her first intellectual property law in 1979 to implement and enforce new regulations, and has gone so far as to create special intellectual property courts with judges specifically trained in the field. This amounts to a twofold recognition that China's other courts are lacking in both efficiency and fairness in this area of legal practice.[9] But we should note that, in truth, what is often termed the "rampant" music piracy rate in China amounts to roughly 85 percent of the recordings in circulation in that country, which is actually less than the estimated 90 percent experienced in the USA.[10]

Not to put too fine a point on it, although China is making some effort to reform her intellectual property law, the Chinese do not have the US's problem of skewed economic perceptions with respect to the various forms of intellectual property. The policy result then is that China puts much greater emphasis on protecting patents and trademarks than on protecting copyrights. This is the opposite of the regulatory and enforcement scheme which has evolved in the US

This may indeed be a natural outcome of the fact that the Chinese are neither submerged in an entertainment infatuated culture, nor the perpetual targets of media lobbyists. But we dare speculate that it may also have something to do with the educational backgrounds of their leadership.

The Chinese leaders are predominately engineers and scientists. Even China's newest leaders, who are known as "technocrats" because they cut their political teeth as bureaucrats in high rise office buildings, are still mostly trained in the hard sciences.[11] This is in contrast to their predecessors who worked in the farm fields and the factories.

Compare this to the educational backgrounds of the US national legislators. The overwhelming majority were trained in the liberal arts or "soft" sciences like political science (i.e. not actually sciences at all). In fact, there are more entertainers and actors in Congress than engineers.[12] Under such circumstances, it should be no surprise when hard knowledge and reality take a back to seat to wishful thinking or childish fantasy. The Chinese wisely recognize that this is not desirable for command or navigation of a ship of state.

While the Chinese leadership's fondness for the hard sciences may have a predictable influence on China's intellectual property policy, it has caused a bit of a snag in the area of computer software regulation. Generally, computer software crosses into the world of IP as a matter of copyright, and, as mentioned, copyrighted material is more or less fair game under China's IP regime. This is true even when the software is of a totally industrial nature (i.e., not a video game). It gets the same lax or nonexistent level of enforcement as the copyrights covering music or video recordings in China.

This is where China's refusal to protect copyrights as a matter of policy is actually recognized as economically damaging. The lack of statutory protection for their industrial software leaves a dangerous hole in their defenses. In response to the dilemma, China is attempting to create a separate type of copyright just for computer software that will (purportedly) be enforced for domestic and foreign entities, equally.[13] (This is in contrast to the United States which as mentioned in chapters 14 and 23 created a patent regime to protect software. But, the overall results for the US have been indifferent at best.)

So for a short analytical recap, let's use our above methodology to predict and understand China's policy with respect to foreign produced DVDs, a case the US recently took before the

World Trade Organization (WTO).[14]  The first point we should take into account is that, as discussed above, DVD piracy does not significantly affect China's economy.  Consequently, we should ask ourselves, "So long as it is not seditious, does China care?"  The answer is, No, they don't."  Chinese artists are given little or no IP protection, so we can hardly expect foreign artists to fare any better.  Accordingly, the outcome of the case was that China resisted incorporation of significant copyright protection for products of the fine arts, and, the WTO, essentially, acquiesced.

See how well the method works?  (And by the way, although the US technically "won" a portion of its lawsuit at the WTO, the West resoundingly lost its case in attempting to force the Chinese to assert criminal sanctions for IP infringement.).[15]

Now, enlightened and properly oriented by all of the above information, try a purely academic exercise.  Ask yourself, "Which nation's IP policies more closely adhere to the IP principles laid out by the US Constitution, those of the US or those of China?"  The answer may surprise you.  But it certainly makes more sense for China.  Since the USA does not appear to take her Constitutional principles seriously in this matter, perhaps it is good that someone else does; Even China.

%%%%%%%%%%%%%%%%%%%%%%%%%%%%%%%%%%%%%%%%

FOOTNOTES

[1] The Chinese dragon is a mythical creature, depicted as a long, scaled, snakelike creature with four claws.  In contrast to the Western dragon which stands on four legs and which is usually portrayed as evil, the Chinese dragon has long been a potent symbol of auspicious power in Chinese folklore and art.  The dragon is sometimes used in the West as a national emblem of China.  This usage within both the People's Republic of China and the Republic of China on Taiwan, however, is rare because of the dragon's historical association with the Emperor of China, starting with the

Yuan Dynasty and then reemerging during the Qing Dynasty as it appeared on national flags, and its aggressive or warlike connotations which the Chinese government wishes to avoid. The cuddly looking giant panda is far more often used within China as a national emblem.

[2] "The Congress shall have Power . . . To promote the Progress of Science and useful Arts, by securing for limited Times to Authors and Inventors the exclusive Right to their respective Writings and Discoveries;" US Const. art. I, § 8, cl. 8.

[3] For a more compete explanation of this matter, see Chapters 16 and 22.

[4] In fact, the US played by largely the same playbook the first hundred years or so of its existence. Not only did the US frequently try to muzzle oppositional "expression" against government policies (remember those Sedition Acts), but Americans were notorious for ignoring copyrights. Only after the economic benefits of copyright protection began to outweigh the benefits of infringement did this country begin to seriously address IP protection. See *"Intellectual Property Protection in China,"* a presentation by David J. Mosser, Mike Curb College of Entertainment & Music Business, Belmont University, Aug. 28, 2008.

[5] There is currently a debate amongst Chinese politicos over which government agency should regulate the online video game World of Warcraft. See "Bureaucrats clash in a bid for absurdity: Two Chinese government agencies are locked in conflict over the regulation of ***World of Warcraft***, Gaston (North Carolina) Gazette, Nov. 19, 2009, available at: **http://gastongazette.com/articles/ Absurdity-40629-bid-bureaucrats.html.**

[6] If one peruses the top ten US exports, music, recordings, movies or videos are nowhere on the chart. In fact, in 2007, number ten on the list was "computer accessories at $29.4 billion. In comparison, DVD tapes and discs came in at a paltry 1/6th of that ($4.9 billion). Top American Exports in 2007 Leading USA Products Include Semiconductors and Civilian Aircraft © Daniel Workman Jul 27, 2008 **http://import-export.suit101.com/article.cfm/topamerican exports in 2007#ixzz0YYy6VbJb**
In the following year's report (2008) DVDs, tapes, and discs did not even merit mention. America's Top Imports & Exports 2008, US Shows Trade Advantages in Civilian Aircraft and Semiconductors, © Daniel Workman, Oct 6, 2009, **http://import-export.suite101.com/article.cfm/americas topimports exports 2008#ixzz0YZ1Rq0Ip**

[7] See Bell, Daniel A., *"China's New Confucianism: Politics and Everyday Life in a Changing Society,"* Princeton Univ. Press, 2008.

[8] Throughout this volume, the word *piracy* repeatedly appears in association with intellectual property matters. We use the term in the title and text merely as convenient or humorous slang. The proper term is *infringement*. To use the word *piracy* may be darkly romantic and perhaps sounds a bit adventurous, but to seriously or formally apply that terminology to such picayune and fuzzily defined activities as mere intellectual property infringement subverts and cheapens the meaning of a serious term for a serious crime. We do it tongue in cheek. It is entertaining, but those who essay to assert it with a straight face to describe intellectual property infringement impinge upon their own credibility.

[9] See: http://www.chinalawblog.com/2009/02/the_wto_chinas_media_copyright.html

[10] *Intellectual Property Protection in China*, a presentation by David J. Mosser, Mike Curb College of Entertainment & Music Business, Belmont University, 1900 Belmont Blvd, Nashville, TN, 37212, 28 August 2008

[11] While there is evidence that this may be starting to change as there are more and more Chinese undergraduates enroll in the soft sciences like law and economics, you will still be hard pressed to find any student majoring in the humanities. This is a matter of national policy. Chinese students have been encouraged for at least the last thirty years to pursue degrees in the hard sciences or technical fields like engineering, chemistry and computer science. See e.g., Liu, Melinda, "China's old guard—engineers like Hu Jintao and Jiang Zemin, and revolutionaries like Mao Zedong and Deng Xiaoping—is giving way to a new breed of Communist Party technocrat." Newsweek Web Exclusive, Sep 8, 2009

[12] *Aviation Week and Space Technology*, Washington Outlook, Entertainment Now, 23 Feb 2009, pg. 21.

[13] See Dickinson, Steve, *"The WTO, China's Media, Copyrights And Other IP. It's A Control Thing,"* Chinalawblog.com, Feb. 9, 2009, available at: http://chinalawblog.com/2009/02/the_wto_chinasmedia_copyright.html

[14] *"China – Measures Affecting the Protection and Enforcement of Intellectual Property Rights: Report of the Panel,"* 26 January 2009, WT/DS362/R.

[15] See Dickinson, *"The WTO, China's Media, Copyrights and Other IP. It's A Control Thing,"* supra; see also Wang, Tina, "US Talks Up WTO Piracy Ruling, But It's All Wind," Forbes Magazine, Jan. 27, 2009.

# 18

# Manufacturing in China

*Pirate's Rule #18: The truth is valuable.
So part with it sparingly.*

      The panda ain't no Teddy bear. When dealing with businesses in China, expect to face the previously expounded two laws of a pirate; "What a man CAN do, and what he CAN'T." Simply assume that your Chinese counterparts know no other law. This will help you to remember to, as mentioned in Chapter 2, "Always cut the cards."

Whether or not you file for a patent in China, if you need bids from Chinese manufacturers to produce your clever doohicky, solicit all the bids simultaneously. Experience has shown that it is not unusual for a Chinese manufacturer to immediately file for a patent on your invention in China, and then try to use that filing to block other bids.[1]   By simultaneously presenting your project to multiple bidders, you set such scoundrels up against each other, and nullify such underhanded efforts.

If possible, keep the identity and details of your product a secret from potential manufacturers--particularly any overseas manufacturer.   If the manufacturers do not know what they are manufacturing, they are greatly handicapped in their efforts to capitalize on pirating it.   In fact, I suggest that you create a misleading name for your project.   For example, if you are manufacturing model plane propellers, take advantage of the fact that they also might serve as components of desk fans.   (Yes, I realize that this suggestion may be a bit off the wall.   But it communicates the spirit of the concept.)   This tactic may apply, at least, in the bidding phase.   When it comes time to import your wares, however, greater descriptive veracity may be in order, due to legal, international trade, importation, and customs issues.

For further security, if your invention has different parts, consider having different manufacturers make the different parts. Avoid having it assembled or packaged outside the United States. This further helps to keep any sneaky sea-weasels from figuring out details of what you are manufacturing, and therefore obstructs efforts to copy it.

Ensure that none of the manufacturers know about the others. This methodology has already been successfully used on many high security projects. For example, in the United States, we understand it was employed to keep the stealth bomber and fighter projects secret, even from the manufacturers.

%%%%%%%%%%%%%%%%%%%%%%%%%%%%%%%%%%%%%%%

FOOTNOTE

[1] In fact, even if you have not sought Chinese business, the mere publication of your patent application may trigger submission of a similar application in China. That Chinese application may be used to extort high manufacturing fees from you. This is a good reason to consider including a nonpublication request in your US-only patent application.

# 19

# The International Market Place

## (Should you seek extra-domestic protection?)

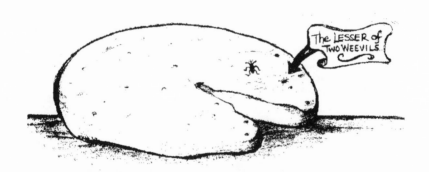

The LESSER of TWO WEEVILS

Pirate's Rule #19: Nobody gets it all (not of even the weevily hardtack).

Acquisition of patent protection in the international arena has become greatly simplified over the last decade or so. The streamlined, and standardized procedures created under the Patent Cooperation Treaty (PCT) are the main reason for this. A single "one size fits all" PCT application can be drafted and examined to create a toe hold for filing patents in just about any other nation on the planet, and it can be prepared relatively inexpensively.

But like a two shilling crocodile for your bathtub, just being cheap does not make it desirable.

Although PCT patent applications may be standardized, there is no such thing as a single, all-encompassing *international patent*. Sooner or later, that "international" PCT application must be submitted to each individual nation wherein protection is desired. And the cost of adding protection in each individual nation will likely approximate the cost of your home country patent application. It matters not whether that nation (or its market share) is as big as a whale, or small as a shrimp, you can expect the costs to be comparable.

So from a business perspective, you must ask yourself one question, "Is it worth it?" If your home market is the US of A, consider the fact that the US market share is far out of proportion with her population size. You may easily find that eighty percent (or more) of the world market for your product lies within the borders of the United States. The remaining one hundred ninety five countries' market share is, then, on the average, about one tenth of a percent each. Of course the actual numbers show significantly disproportionate concentrations in a few nations. All the same, how much would you pay to get that last twenty percent, given that each additional national patent will cost about the same as your US patent? Further, could you afford to defend your patents overseas, even if you got them? Is it worth the investment? Frequently, the answer is, "Very likely not."

Talking hypothetical numbers, let's say you can get US patent protection for your invention totally tied up for a price of $10,000. Let's say that with that, you have covered 80 percent of the potential market. To get patent protection in, say ten additional nations, will likely cost $10,000 each. But for your hundred thousand bucks, you do *not* cover the rest of the world market, but only a few more percent of it.

Clearly, we have ventured into the realm of fast diminishing returns. We will run out of money before we run out of countries. It is time to order all engines back full, before we get sucked into the maelstrom.

I generally advise my US small entrepreneur clients to forego the expenses of international patent protection, unless they have a product that is particularly specific to a region outside the US, or unless they have licensees lined up and ready to assume responsibility for achieving patent prosecution in their own regions. On the other hand, if my clients are outside the USA, I generally advise them to add the United States to their list of nations for which patent protection is sought. It is the best deal around.

# 20

# Selling That License

*Pirate's Rule # 20: Hit hard, hit fast, hit often.*

*(Admiral William F. "Bull" Halsey)*

# Making the Pitch

When it comes to licensing your invention, take a lesson from songwriters. When a writer pitches a song, he simply plays it. He does not dwell on the manner in which he got the idea for the lyrics. He does not expound and extol the ingenious combination of time signatures and key changes he created.

He knows that (as 'is Lordship, the good Duke Ellington always said) "If it *sounds* good, it *is* good." And that is all anybody in the commercial market cares about. (Well, Rap "music" excluded. It's the exception that proves the rule.)

Your potential invention licensee or buyer, has the same sentiments. Demonstrate the product. If your invention will clearly become an essential item, then the buyer cares not a whit about the miraculous events leading to its creation. He has little interest in the details of its mysterious workings. What the potential licensee wants first and foremost is plain and simple. He wants a product that gives him a grossly disproportionate advantage over the competition. Your job is to show him how your invention can do that.

If you want to get the attention of potential licensees, boldly use the words "unfair advantage." That is music to their ears. (If you recognize a piratical smell about all this, remember that it is the profit motive that drives pirates, the same as other businessmen. A mere profit motive is obviously not inherently evil, of itself.)

# An Example

Let me offer an example of the principle in action, drawn from my own days as a techno-pirate. My cohorts and I arranged to exploit a clever combination of satellite channels, telephone switches, transatlantic cables, and microcomputers to extend top quality, high volume, low cost, data and voice communications into areas where present quality was poor, availability was limited, and cost was exorbitant.[1]

The details of our system were a bit complex, but using it was simple. This was in the early days of cellphone technology. To prepare for my sales meeting, I equipped myself with a cellphone and programmed some necessary access codes into it. Then, I went to meet our potential client. My pitch included no technical brief. I had no slide presentation. There was no glitzy video. All I did was pull out my cellphone, press one button, and hand the phone to my potential licensee. Then I said, "Listen for the tone, and dial anywhere in the world. Anywhere. It will cost one-tenth of what you pay, now.

This worked, consistently. Customers understood it every time. They clearly and instantaneously saw why they needed my product. It promised them the proverbial and prized "unfair advantage." They could not resist and the whole task took only seconds.

Admittedly, not all technologies lend themselves to such presentations. But the character of your presentation should always be tailored to achieve this sort of instantly discernible message.

We concentrated on acquiring customers such as hotels that would generate high resale demand for our products. Our pitch simply included that fact that we could plug our capability into hotel switchboards, permitting all their international guests to automatically share the benefit of our service. The hotels could independently set service resale prices to their guests, and choose their own profit margins. Thus they could save money not only for themselves, but also for their guests. Although we certainly did not turn away individual single item buyers, the targets we kept centered in our sights were these long-term high resale volume customers each of whom would generate sales of hundreds or thousands of units of my product.

## The Contract

Now, with respect to preparing the license contract; "Brevity is the soul of wit," so sayeth the bard. Go for simplicity. Do not let your attorney "lawyer it to death." License agreements can easily get out of hand in complexity. Do not let this happen.

The single license contract of which I am most proud was drafted under the watchful eye and direct intervention of an inventor himself. At his direction, the only formula or equation contained therein was a one to one ratio. It said, essentially, "For every unit manufactured, you pay me a flat fee, specified herein. For this privilege, you will also pay me a reasonable advance, also specified herein, to defray my expenses and compensate me for my efforts up to now."

This was a stroke of genius. He negotiated a non-refundable advance, and a simple flat fee per unit. His method eliminated wrestling with delivery issues, discount calculations, returns, sliding scales, or sales ratios. In fact, the contract required no calculation of royalty *percentages* at all. Not only was the whole thing clean and uncomplicated, it promised quick, inexpensive audits in the future. Most attractive.

My client walked in with this contract in hand. He walked out with the contract signed, and a check attached. Scheduled for only a ten minute appointment, he was invited to stay for lunch, and dinner, and had a return invitation. The estimated value of his signed contract was over one hundred million dollars (for my client, not for me).

%%%%%%%%%%%%%%%%%%%%%%%%%%%%%%%%%%%%%
FOOTNOTE

[1] We were called *"pirates"* only because this trod on toes of incompetent government monopolies. That title was fine by us.

120

# 21

# Boxing the Compass
## (The Inventor's Mini-MBA)

Pirate's Rule #21:  Inventing is but
a small part of innovation.

One of the first lessons for every apprentice seaman was known as "boxing the compass." He had to memorize all the thirty-two points of the compass by proper title, and rattle them off on command. And he had to literally "learn the ropes." Learning the ropes can be a rough challenge for every new hand. The same applies to new small businessmen. But it is extremely important to have a handle on such basics *before* you head for the deep water, alone. Here are a few key lessons to get you started.

## ❋YOUR BUSINESS GOAL

The main goal of a business is (drum roll) to ***stay in business***. Note here that we did not say your goal is *profits*. Neither did we assert that planetary wellbeing is the proper first calling of your enterprise. This may seem a bit tangential approach, but in choosing your sailing tack, the best speed is made on an oblique course, cutting a wide swath *across* the wind. Business works the same way.

Profits are a good and necessary thing, but if you point your bow directly at the immediate profit destination, you may find that you lose headway. In the longer term, profits are absolutely necessary. But pursuit of maximized short term gains can become commercial suicide.

We do love increased share values. Dividends for shareholders are grand. "Improvement of the planet" is warm and fuzzy. But if you can create and preserve a successful commercial enterprise, then in that, alone, you have accomplished a great thing. You have benefitted us all. If your enterprise produces jobs, and *preserves* them, you are doing plenty for shareholders, public wellbeing, and the planet in general.

Establish your business and *stay in business*. That is a substantial goal of itself. The rest is gravy. So keep in mind that, whatever you do, preserving your business is your first priority. Livelihoods of many other people may depend on it. Other goals must be evaluated, configured, or sacrificed as necessary to serve this priority.

### ❀WHY BEGIN?

The only viable grounds for starting any new business are *significant economic advantage.* (Don't leave home without it.) How do you identify a "significant economic advantage"? Just imagine an advantage that feels unfair, but isn't. That's the kind of advantage I mean. Your new intellectual property is the source of your advantage. (As such, it is the heart and soul of your enterprise. Protect it accordingly.) And, if your advantage is technological, remember that *no technological advantage is permanent.*[1] Always be in search of the next one. You will need it to stay in business.

### ❀MEETING DEMAND

The number one cause of small business failure is *failure to meet demand.* Contrary to what you might expect, most failure is emphatically not due to *insufficient* demand. Fail to fill an order once, and you probably will not get a second chance. Failure to meet demand, today, becomes the primary cause of insufficient demand, tomorrow.

### ❀PATENTS

Patents don't protect inventions any more than hunting licenses bag turkeys. The patent just declares open season and gives you permission to hunt infringers. Remember that *hunting can get expensive.*

### ❀TRADEMARKS

Choose your trademark carefully. Give wide berth to trademarks owned by others. Failure to do either of these can run you up on surprisingly destructive rocks and shoals.

123

# ❀TRADE SECRETS

Your business is *your* business and nobody else's. Never miss a good chance to shut up about stuff that is only *your business.*

# ❀COPYRIGHTS

Copyright is governed by statutes clearly constructed by word weasels. Do not depend on them for much protection. (This does create great job security for some lawyers, though.) Be aware that the moment you create a copyrightable work it is in fact under copyright. But in the US you cannot defend that copyright until you register it. So if you want a defendable copyright, get off yer soggy scuttlebutt, have the thing properly registered, and be done with it. The job should not be expensive to accomplish. Copyright registration costs less than a keg of stale hardtack.

# ❀NONDISCLOSURE and NONCOMPETE AGREEMENTS

Absolutely essential. Always. Under all circumstances. Use them, but don't trust them. (Take my word on this.) And remember that they can never, ever, take the place of a filed patent application, or of a patent. All the same, to the courts a Nondisclosure Agreement is one important proof that you are properly protecting your trade secrets and other confidential business information. This is no small matter. (But, you do NOT need one for your patent attorney.)

# ❀WORK

Getting an invention to the market is work, lots of work. There is no Suez or Panama Canal, nor Northwest Passage to get 'round it. Patents, trademarks, and copyrights are not roads to easy money. They're just tools with which to perform your mission.

# ⚜LICENSING and ROYALTIES

With respect to selling the rights to your invention, or keeping them all to yourself, note that 10 percent royalty on the profits from 10,000 units sold beats 100 percent of the profits on 10 units sold. (A thousand doubloons beat ten). And it has infinitely fewer headaches. If you have not manufacturing, distribution, and business management experience and resources, seriously consider licensing your creation to somebody who does. Very seriously. A mere dinghy sailor may own a mighty ship. But a wise one knows when to hire it out to a capable master and crew.

# ⚜INTERNATIONAL MARKET

The lion's share of the world market for most new intellectual property is located *inside the US borders*. Furthermore, patent protection in the US is less expensive than anywhere else in the world. So weigh carefully the extravagant cost of patent protection *outside* the US. It may not be a sensible investment.

If ninety percent, or eighty percent, or seventy percent, of your market is in the US, you probably can afford to blow off the rest like foam from your beer. Though, of course, if you follow good business practices, (as taught herein) you also can probably get most of the leftovers, too, even without a patent outside the US.

# ⚜MARKETING

Build a better mousetrap, and......in truth, nobody is likely to notice or care. The world will emphatically NOT beat a path to your door. Only poets or fools assert, otherwise...and poets don't sell mousetraps.

Quite the contrary, once you have created that better mousetrap you must flog it for all you are worth. Sell, sell, sell. Draw your saber and hack a path to every door, hatch, or portal where potential customers or licensees may await. Jam a marlinspike in the door hinge and make your pitch. Refer to Pirate's Rule #20; Hit hard. Hit fast. Hit often.

## ❀ HIRED MARKETING

Hired marketing may have some limited place for small entrepreneurs. But it tends to be prohibitively expensive, and most new inventors do not have a great reserve of currency. Marketers seldom work for only a percentage of the take. Generally, they demand recompense, whether or not they successfully market your product.

In response to this situation, not one of my own *successful* clients has, so far, contracted for his marketing. And, remember, I have an inordinate number of successful clients. In view of this, we deduce that if you are smart enough to be a good inventor, you are danged sure smart enough to market your own inventions. (Keep in mind that you may most wisely market your invention for *licensing*. See LICENSING and ROYALTIES, above.) There's no unequivocal need to pay some slick land lubber, or clueless weasel-wording, marketing poet to do it for you. (But it does not hurt to read Orville Redenbacher's successful popcorn marketing story. He did pay for marketing advice (once). But he did his own marketing. And you can learn from his experience.)

## ❀ INTERNET MARKETING AND WEBSITES

The Internet is magic, but Internet sales are not. Merely making your product available online, or advertising it online, is not a means of instant success. So do not go overboard investing in Internet operations without careful study and thought.

## ❀ BILLION DOLLAR IDEAS

Yes, Virginia, there really are billion dollar ideas. But there are also million dollar ideas, and hundred thousand dollar ideas, and tiny niche market ideas. Each level requires a different approach to marketing, finance, and production. One size does not fit all. Do not let some bum-boating Shanghai sea snake oil salesman bamboozle you into investing a million doubloons in a hundred shilling idea.

## ❀ FINANCE

Borrowed money costs more than cash. Far more. Period. If it didn't, banks would not loan money. (After all, what other reason is there, Christian charity and good will? If you buy that, shipmate, I've got a trained sea bat to show you.) Credit cards, unless fully paid off monthly adding no interest, fall under this heading. Do not get me started on this. As a new inventor, expect your profit margins to be so thin you can use them for oil paper windows. Do not expect much freeboard for loading on loan expenses.

## ❀ CASH FLOW

Small phrase, big subject, too big to properly cover here. For now, just remember that money owed to you does not pay bills you owe. You must be "on target, on time." In the real world, merely dropping your shot on a given target at any old time is insufficient. Timing is everything. "Too late'" can spell disaster. Understand this and remain acutely aware of its importance. It will help you avoid biting off more than you can chew.

## ❀ THE MONEY DEMON

Get this sea devil under control from the very start. Both misers and spendthrifts are subject to the same nasty demon. Both are ruled by money, and both are miserable.

This fiend has a weak point, though. Turn loose of him, rightly, and he turns loose of you. But as in the case of the sailor who got a tiger shark by the tail, learning the right way to turn loose is important.

Here is how to start. Up front, and right off the top of every pay packet, set aside a bit of silver for somebody who needs it more than you do. And when you see that need, fill it. There are plenty of places to aim: churches, schools, shelters, food banks. As an unabashed seafarer, I have a natural predilection toward occasionally shipping some doubloons to an outfit called Mercy Ships. Some of my old reformed shipmates are accomplishing things with that crew that'll warm even the heart of Davy Jones himself.[2]

As for how much to dole out, shoot for a measly dime on the dollar; A buck from every ten. You won't feel it. Really, you won't. But it will be Godsend to the person who needs it. You *will* feel good about it. But more important, you will find that you have less compulsion to spend. You'll want less. Your material priorities will better fall into place. The money demon will be marooned far over the horizon. (This is a lesson true diehard pirates never seem to learn.)

Like the wind in my sails, this is a mystery. I cannot see it. But I know it works. Experience does not lie. Trust me, try it, and when you prove for yourself how true it is, pass it along to the next greenhorn.

%%%%%%%%%%%%%%%%%%%%%%%%%%%%%%%%%%%%%%
FOOTNOTES

[1] "Intellectual property has the shelf life of a banana." Bill Gates (perhaps apocryphal).

[2] You can find Mercy Ships online at **www.mercyships.org**. Be sure to tell'em I sent you. And if you *really* want an adventure, sign on with them for a bit. Short duty tours on board are available for just about any job you'd care to do.[*] Their business plan is to provide you with an adventurous working vacation. The concept

cannot be beat.  After some folks arrive, they simply cannot bring themselves to leave.

In the alternative, the Salvation Army gets great bang for your buck, too.  You will find them dug in at **http://www.salvation armyusa.org/usn/www usn 2.nsf**.  They really know how to squeeze the milk of human kindness out of every doubloon, even if they are saltless land lubbers.

*Except they do not have slots for pirates or lawyers onboard.  Of course, it rather goes without saying that they do not knowingly sail with pirates in the crew.  However they are, in fact, quite explicit about not signing on lawyers.  One cannot imagine why.

# 22
# Required; Adult Supervision for IP Legislation

**Pirate's Rule #22: In Washington, tinsel trumps treasure.**

*(with contributions by Tracy Kane, Esq.)*

"Authority without wisdom is like a heavy axe without an edge: fitter to bruise than to polish."[1] By the look of it, US Patent, Trademark and Copyright legislation is suffering from a deficit of adult quality supervision. Really. Now, if our present statutory structure were the product of a junior high civics class project, we could understand how it got into its present condition. If a fourteen-year-old music groupie estimated the economic and social value of the latest hit song to be superior to that of, for example, a new AIDS vaccine, we might yet forgive her youthful exuberance.

But when a bunch of middle-aged to ancient legislators demonstrate these same sentiments, we can only wonder at their childish and frivolous priorities. And we have plenty of cause to wonder, for in present intellectual property legislation, frivolity soundly trumps progress and productivity. Tinsel trumps treasure. So, instead of advancing *with* the law, we are largely forced to advance *in spite of it.*

As a point of comparison, we can look to an example recently made famous on the silver screen.[2] In this case, a big bully automobile manufacturer (even before the bailout era) absconded with a new and immensely valuable patented automobile technology, (windshield wipers), and no government entity voluntarily intervened. This is, in fact, the way our system functions. In contrast, if my cabin boy downloads bootleg copies of Beatles® music originally recorded 30 years ago, he can GO TO JAIL.[3] It's nuts, but that is also how our system functions.

You see, should the rightful owner of a mechanical technology (like the windshield wipers) want his patent rights defended, the task falls on his shoulders, alone. ***His hard earned patent amounts to little more than a hunting license.*** He alone must detect, locate, and apprehend the malefactors. He alone must file suit (and absorb the astronomical upfront costs) to get the malefactors into court. And for all that, his patent protection lasts only about 20 years (and effectively, even less). This is great news for potential pirates, because all the really valuable and important stuff gets little protection, compared to the pure frivolity of music and videos.

Compare this with the copyright system. Owners of the copyrights need not lift a finger in defense of even their most vain or inconsequential creations. They need not file suit, nor pay for the proceedings. The owners need not even find or identify infringing offenders. This is because copyright infringement is the subject of *criminal statutes*. The injured party need not pursue the criminal prosecution, nor even approve of it or be aware of it.

*I am not making this up!*[4]

Remember the intimidating copyright warning at the opening screen displays of your DVDs? Remember the part about "criminal penalties"?[5] The publishers are actually saying these things with a straight face. The more frivolous the intellectual property subject matter, it seems, the more onerous the penalties for "infringing" them. "Fair and balanced" regulation of intellectual property disappeared long ago.[6]

As mentioned above, putting this in analogous terms, a patent is the practical equivalent of a twenty-year hunting license. That being said, if a patent is the practical equivalent of a temporary hunting license, then a copyright is the practical equivalent of a statute that tasks the game warden with hunting turkeys for you, bagging them, bringing them home for you and roasting them for you.....*forever.*[7]

I am sure that there are folks who approve of this present arrangement, but not necessarily *sane* ones...Well, not sane *mature* folks, anyway. So since nobody else is apparently taking the trouble, metaphorically speaking, to offer a bit of adult guidance for the kids legislating out Washington way, we shall take the chalk and jot a couple of lessons onto the nearest bulkhead. Feel free to copy them down in your cuffs for later reference.

**LESSON #1:** <u>**THE REALITY**</u>

The reality is that music is lucky to have any statutory protection at all, much less protection in perpetuity, and inclusion under criminal statutes. Our intellectual property law (with the exception of trademarks) is purely a child of arbitrary statute. It comes not from the tradition of Common Law, but purely from the meddling hands of legislators, "from scratch."[8] Thus, it, is not part of our "certain inalienable" and "self-evident" rights.

However, our intellectual property law does, indeed, originate in the US Constitution. Article I, Section 8, Paragraph 8, proclaims, "Congress shall have power . . . to promote the progress of ***science and useful arts***, by securing for limited times to ***authors and inventors*** the exclusive right to their respective ***writings and discoveries***." (emphasis added).

Now those words are quite precise. But if we read them in a sloppy manner, we get sloppy results. So, let's peruse them with some discipline. The authors deserve at least that.

Since our issue is with music, let us first examine the term "useful arts." "Useful arts" are not "fine arts." This is a significant distinction. "Art" in the language of our Constitution, is the domain of the "inventor," not the "artist." In 1789, when that fine document was penned, "art" meant what we term today to be "technology."[9]

Continuing to follow this paragraph in our Constitution, the word "science" was, back then, used to mean what we would now more commonly term "knowledge." So authors do not give us "art." Quite in the contrary, authors give us "science" (knowledge). T'is the inventors who give us "useful arts."

Upon reflection, we can see how this all makes good sense. It is confirmed by the parallel construction of the sentences. Lining

133

up this parallel construction, we note again that "science" comes from "authors" and "arts" are those creations brought to us by "inventors." The order of the following terms "writings and discoveries" nails it for us. Reading the meaning any other way stretches credulity, and ignores both the contemporary dictionary and the excellent composition skills of the drafters. The subsequent "dumbing down" of our language to confuse "fine art" with "useful arts" does not retroactively change the meaning of the document.

So again, we point out, so far as intellectual property law is concerned, *authors do not give us "art" and by extension neither do composers nor performers*. The only authors' products specified for protection are those that give us "knowledge." In view of this, does anybody see a slot in this plan for, say, Lady Gaga, by virtue of her performances giving us "knowledge"? Me neither. Can anybody imagine the founding fathers enacting legislation to clamp down on the activities of wandering minstrels to restrict the free exchange of music and poetry? Me neither.

So how did fine arts get added to our formerly palatable copyright brew? Well, it was the result of a statute wheedled into existence several years after the Constitution was ratified. It was created, apparently, in response to a court decision wherein one circuit Justice Thompson, reading with remarkable clarity, reasoned that copyright is created to promote "science" (knowledge) such as would be found in the fixed character of a book, but not to promote mere "industry" as more properly describes the ephemeral character of a newspaper. Such time sensitive writings would be utterly obsolete before copyright registration could even be accomplished. Therefore, he reasoned, newspapers and their content, being of the most temporary nature, were not eligible for copyright registration.[10]

This precipitated, in an apparent effort to mimic the English copyright structure in retrograde, an act (4 Stat. 436 (1831)) that gave, among other things, books, maps, charts and *music compositions* 28 years of monopolistic rights for their creators. Further, it gave right of renewal for another 14 years.

By this single broad stroke, they added a huge cargo of freeloaders, and tripled the previous period of legal monopoly. The legislators and their progeny, having established precedent, never looked back. They, bless their lobbied little hearts, just thirstily keep returning to the jug for another swig. Each time, it seems they make the system more complex and convoluted, further enriching middlemen and prying profits out of authors, composers, and performers, all while claiming to further protect those same authors, composers and inventors.

The bid now stands at lifetime plus seventy years.[11] Thus under the present statutes, the average copyright would easily last for over a century, most of it after the author dies. So, referring back to the constitutional basis for copyright, *we have created a system for encouraging creativity from dead men.* This benefits neither the creators nor the society at large. It merely enriches whomsoever bought or inherited their legal gravy train. But even with all this, of course, there is little reason to believe that the present provisions will not be again rendered moot by yet another term extension.

It seems authors, composers, and performers consistently get snookered into supporting enactment of these legislative monsters. This is like being persuaded to act as Kraken feed. There is not much of an "up" side to it. While many authors, and artists militantly stand ready to defend their ships against boarders, they already have pirates aboard tucked away in their own berthing quarters.

In view of the above, we might offer a bit of advice to our indignant bellyachers of the entertainment industry. Do not get too carried away with asserting the righteousness of your complaints and legislative demands. Somebody might notice the linguistic loophole ya'll slipped through and set about plugging it. Be aware that such sentiments are not unheard of. Quoting a popular movie from days long past, "This is just *radio!*"[12]

Like any other leisure activity indulging the entertainments can quickly become too expensive. You will most certainly find that many nondomestic governments consider your indignity beyond comprehension and essentially unworthy of any recognition except lip service. Not all members of the world community can or want to afford such frivolity. Do not expect this to significantly change. Not ever. In evidence, we offer the mass slap down of the SOPA ("Stop Online Piracy Act) that occurred in early 2012. This gave the US legislatures a lesson they never should have needed in the first place. Expect more of the same if that lesson needs repeated.

And for those compulsive social manipulators whose little brains instantly start wrestling with this inequity between entertainment and technology by envisioning even more legislation, "NO, the answer is *not* to add criminal penalties to patent law." Take my word for it, few patent attorneys are interested in undertaking or defending endless, frivolous, and nonproductive criminal prosecutions. However, nobody else has the necessary technical skill or education to undertake that bit of futility. Legislators, please keep your mitts off this status quo, thank you very much. The fix for bad medicine is not more bad medicine. The patient already has acquired the glassy eyed symptoms of over medication.[13]  More patent regulations are not the answer. That would merely generate more cause for litigation, precisely as the frivolous copyright statutes do.[14]

Like Rumpole's legal aid briefs, additional criminal statutes may provide some degree of security for wayward litigators, but they facilitate no progress, culturally, intellectually, or scientifically.

## LESSON #2 THE CHOICE

In view of current technology, our legislators have reached the point that they face two options in the world of copyright:

1. Get real.

*or*

2. Become irrelevant (or *more* irrelevant)

The first option is simple. Proverbially, the simple things are always hard. These realities are, indeed, an inconvenient truth.[15] So we have largely ignored the first option. Falling by default into the second option merely results in generation of a plethora of litigation which is, in practical terms, meaningless.[16] However, this is what has happened. In real terms, much of our IP statutes are of no more consequence than is the honking of the old flightless barnyard gander as he attempts to influence the wild geese soaring overhead. The flyers ignore him and his pitiful honking. They have places to go and things to accomplish, and simply cannot be bothered with irrelevant visions of self-proclaimed command and authority.

## LESSON #3 THE REMEDY

The remedy for our nonsensical situation is to get real with intellectual property law, particularly copyright law. Presently, the tail is already trying to wag the dog. However, except in the fantasies of legislators, lobbyists, and a bag full of Britney-act-alikes, the dog ain't budging.

Employing a previous real world analogy in our own species, we old codgers remember when it seemed that every truck and car on the road was fitted with a two way CB ("Citizens Band") radio. In those days, all radio operators were statutorily required to comply the bureaucratic red tape of applying for and acquiring a radio license prior to transmitting there first "Smokey reports," good buddy. The public response to this statutory requirement was overwhelming. They absolutely ignored it in droves of apocalyptic scale.[17] As soon as the instantly popular radio technology became available, the outdated "law" (mere statute) established to restrict it became irrelevant. The statutes served no recognizable purpose. They were annoying, and there was no means of consistent enforcement available.

Having not the strength of reason, nor of moral authority, nor of coercion, the regulations effectively ceased to exist (although they are still on the books). The rule makers found their rules as irrelevant as the honking of our flightless barnyard goose. However, those purportedly in power do not seem to recognize this repetitive and futile pattern. They apparently think they can cow the crowd into submission. Although "you can't sue them all," the author was assured by a representative of the Copyright Office, "We are happy to try!" I suppose it does provide bureaucratic job security.

The truth is that with ninety percent of the recorded music presently in circulation having been acquired via extralegal means, this irrelevance poses not a mere threat nor even a clear danger. It is a reality. The old recording industry way is not coming back. Understand clearly, this is not a moral pronouncement. We are not advocating this turn of events. Our opinion would not matter anyway. We are simply recognizing the present reality in order to deal with it realistically.

Intellectual property law is a free market issue. No mere legislation has a chance of relevance unless it conforms to public perceptions of what is, at least, reasonable. But the public has long lost favorable perception or even understanding of our IP legal environment. It will not be recovered until these yipping little statutory excuses for law get properly corralled and disciplined. For sure, more statutes are not the answer. And more lawsuits based on already essentially irrelevant statutes are not the answer, either.[18] By now it should be apparent that attempts to coerce the public into compliance with usurious industry dictates are not the answer. That sword is, indeed, two edged. One would best not take it up "lest the righteous seize upon it and tear it from our self-bloodied grasp."[19, 20]

%%%%%%%%%%%%%%%%%%%%%%%%%%%%%%%%%%%%%%%%%%

FOOTNOTES

[1] Bradstreet, Anne. *"Meditations Divine and Moral." The Works of Anne Bradstreet. Ed. Jeannine Hensley. Cambridge: Belknap Press, 1967. 274.* Our beloved colonial American poet, Anne is one of the few authors whom we can reasonably assume to be OUT of copyright. But we would be wrong. She is not; well, not entirely, anyway.

[2] *Flash of Genius*, Universal Studios (2008) (based on the true story of college professor and part time inventor, Robert Kearns', long battle with the US automobile industry to enforce his patent for the design of the intermittent windshield wiper).

[3] Can I say that, or is "GO TO JAIL" a trademark of Milton Bradley?

[4] Can I say, "I am not making this up!" or is that phrase already trademarked by Dave Barry?

[5] *"The unauthorized reproduction or distribution of this copyrighted work is illegal. Criminal copyright infringement, including infringement without monetary gain, is investigated by the FBI and is punishable by up to five years in federal prison and a fine of $250,000."* (I suppose this warning is also under copyright, but we will take a chance and recite it, anyway.)

[6] Can I say "fair and balanced," or is it already trademarked by Fox News?...Oooops, sorry, we've already settled that question. But it had to go to federal court. See footnote 16, below.

[7] For those nit pickers who studiously point out that copyrights are in truth statutorily valid only for the lifetime of the owner, plus seventy years, I respectfully submit that faced with the dread appellation of beloved cartoon characters entering the public domain, Congress, bless their lobbied little hearts, keeps extending copyright terms. This is merely further proof that Mickey Mouse® has, as suspected, acquired significant influence over the US legislature.

[8] *Wheaton v. Peters*, 33 U.S. (8 Pet.) 591 (1834).

[9] If you do not believe me, look it up yourself. All you need is Sam Johnson's dictionary. Copies are still available. (Webster did not venture into dictionary writing until a few decades after Mr. Johnson.) As a matter of parallel interest, this distinction is, we deduce, the reason that a "college of arts and sciences" does not normally include departments for music or literature. These are found, instead, in the colleges of "fine art." A college of "arts and sciences" is for "technology and knowledge." Neat, huh? This understanding also sheds a whole new light on, and beautifully clarifies, the old expression, "...more an art than a science."

[10] *Clayton v. Stone*, 5 F. Cas. 999, 2 Paine 382, 1 US Law Int. 69 (C.C.N.Y. 1829).

[11] *See* Digital Millennium Copyright Act (Pub.L. 105-304, Oct. 28, 1998, 112 Stat. 2860), also known as the Sonny Bono, Mickey Mouse Act. "A hard act to follow."

[12] General Taylor, *Good Morning Vietnam*, Touchstone Pictures (1987).

[13] See the proposed "Orphaned Works Act." First we created a legal environment in which copyrights last so long that the owners become lost in the haze of antiquity, and we confer copyrights without registration. Then to rectify the fact that nobody can legally reproduce the subject material, nor license it, because they cannot find the copyright owners and get permission, our legislators declaim even MORE statutes in an attempt to untangle their own mess by adding to it. This is an absurd situation for statutes purposed to "encourage advancement in the useful arts and science."

[14] Performance rights versus synchronization rights is an example that jumps immediately to mind. Under these provisions, one may be permitted to include a piece of music in a movie, for a certain price ("performance rights"), but if characters in the movie dance along with the tune, an additional fee is demanded ("synchronization rights"). Performance rights also mandate music license fees for those who own restaurants, bars, inns or other such establishment, and for entertainment employ recorded music or videos, have live performers, or even merely play the radio or TV. These fees are collected by Performance Rights Organizations known as ASCAP, BMI, and SESAC. Take care, for they have covert agents checking up on you.

[15] Can I say "inconvenient truth" or does Albert Gore, Jr. already have it trademarked? (OK, OK, so I've overworked that gag.)

[16] *See Louis Vuitton Malletier S.A. v. Haute Diggity Dog, LLC*, 507 F.3d 252 (4th Cir. 2007) (challenging use of "Chewy

Vuitton" in line of dog accessories); *Fox News Network, LLC v. Penguin Group (USA), Inc.*, 2003 WL 23281520 (S.D.N.Y. Aug. 20, 2003) ("Fair and Balanced" Trademark dispute); *V Secret Catalogue, Inc. v. Moseley*, 259 F.3d 464 (6th Cir. 2001) (challenging use of "Victor's Little Secret"); *Lenz v. Universal Music Corp.*, 572 F.Supp.2d 1150 (N.D.Cal. 2008)(User of Internet posting Website filed action alleging that copyright owner acted in bad faith by issuing takedown notice without proper consideration of fair use doctrine in violation Digital Millennium Copyright Act).

[17] "License? We don't need no stinkin' license!" *Butch Cassidy and the Sundance Kid*, Twentieth Century-Fox Film Corporation. (1969).

[18] The recording industry has apparently begun to recognize the futility of attempting to sue their own customers *en masse* and has recently begun teaming up with Internet providers in an attempt to get somebody else to do their dirty work. The goal is to get Internet service providers to intercept apparent pirates by arbitrarily cutting off service to their own customers based on assumed illegal downloading. Imagine what a litigious mess this may become. *See* Sandoval, Greg, *RIAA drops lawsuits; ISPs to battle file sharing*, CNET News, Dec. 18, 2008, available at **http://news.cnet.com /8301-1023 3-10126914-** 93.html.

[19] Good quote, huh? On point and sounds impressively Shakespearian. But there is no need to attribute it because I just made it up. "He who does not quote is not quoted." (Rudyard Kipling) But then, Kipling had never met Yogi Berra. Yogi gets quoted a lot, and he always made up his own stuff. So quote yourself, sez I and get the best of both worlds.

[20] For those who might question the propriety of my quotations delivered without specific permission from publishers, I believe they fall under the "fair use" exception. However, the mere fact that anyone might seriously entertain such a picayune question is indicative of the absurd level of collective conditioning we've undergone. *De minimus non-curate lex.* Move out of your parent's basement and get a life.

*This chapter is adapted from an article originally published by* Nashville Bar Journal *and was drafted with the valuable assistance of Attorney Tracy Kane, who, in a past life, was an international business consultant with particular expertise in China. Now a member of the Nashville Bar, she is a former judicial clerk for the Honorable Richard H. Dinkins. Although she may possess piratical tendencies, she has, to the best of our knowledge, no familial connection with* The Kane Mutiny.

## 23

# We're Harmonizing
## with the
# Wrong Sea Chantey
### (International Harmonization of
### Intellectual Property Statutes)

*Pirate's Rule #23: If it ain't broke,
don't jury-rig it.*

This is another unadulterated seaman's rant, except for omission of the traditional sailor's vocabulary. It seems to this grouchy old deckhand that the US of A is steering a foolish course with respect to intellectual property in general.

Ongoing federal intellectual property legislation has been largely rationalized by a purported need for "harmonization" with the larger world community. Most recently, this harmonization has been primarily directed toward copyright statutes.[1] But, the US patent system has also come under assault.

Acceptance is a universal human desire. People and nations have an inexplicable compulsion to "fit in" and be like everybody else. Further, the United States faces international peer pressure re-enforcing this compulsion to conform. This outside peer pressure is not exerted in the best interests of our nation.

For the US copyright system which already has functional problems, the primary effects of this "harmonization" will only act to exacerbate our problems. The unbalanced copyright monster just continues to grow more top heavy, even though it is already unable to stand on its own, and merely results in apathy toward the out of control statutes.

One feature of our contemplated harmonization concerns royalties for performance rights. It would mandate that recording artists be paid when their recordings are played for a public audience. Up to now US radio broadcasters have not been required to pay royalties for playing music. However, generally speaking, in the rest of the world (with the huge exception of China) broadcasters are required to "pay for play." Since US broadcasters have not paid royalties to copyright holders for any performances, domestic or foreign, foreign stations in retribution have not paid royalties to US copyright holders. Some US copyright holders militate to change this.

International peer pressure and domestic lobby efforts by the entertainment industry are focused on giving the *holders of copyrights for* US recording artists the benefit of royalty payments for radio play. Their proposed statutes require radio broadcast operators pay royalties to copyright holders, including foreign holders, for broadcasting music.

Europeans love this plan, for the US market is several times the size of the market in Europe. Access to this huge US market would be a major windfall. Since, the US market for any intellectual property is many times larger than that of any other nations, the net effect of this arrangement can lead to negative cash flow into US coffers. If we all conformed, for every buck coming into the United States, many more would go out.[2]

Therefore so far as the US economy is concerned, such "harmonization" makes no financial sense. (This is not rocket science.) It may bring in a bit more cash to certain noisy special interest groups[3] But it will do so at comparatively significant expense to most Americans.

For the nation at large, this is not a good deal.

Furthermore, the US copyright system is already far *out* of harmony with the rest of US intellectual property law, which is the envy of the planet. Not surprisingly the US copyright program is not working out very smoothly. The system under which the Copyright Office functions is not properly adapted to accommodate today's vastly increased volume of intellectual property rights. Frankly, the Copyright Office is buried. It needs infrastructure, technology, and manpower. To get these, it needs funds. A quick external perusal identifies the likely cause of their monetary shortfall and suggests an easy fix.

They are short on bucks because not enough money is coming in.[4] This is because unlike the architectures supporting the other major intellectual property matters (patents and trademarks), the Copyright Office derives comparatively little financial support from the people who employ its services.

Let us compare copyright fees to those required to support other intellectual property. A patent application costs at a minimum many hundreds or thousands of dollars in government fees alone. As the application is examined, additional significant fees will often be required. Then, after the patent is granted, maintenance fees of no small sum are demanded every few years. If the fees are not paid, the patent becomes abandoned and enters the public domain making its technology free to all of us for taking.

Likewise, a trademark application requires a fee of, at a minimum, hundreds of dollars. And after the trademark is granted, further costly maintenance is demanded without which the trademark is pronounced "dead." Also note that a non-US patent or trademark has no validity in the US. If you want US benefit, royalties or protections, you must pay US registration and maintenance fees.

As a result, the United States Patent and Trademark Office has for decades generated more revenue than it consumes.[5] And we know precisely which patents or trademarks in this country are dead and which ones are alive, and we know who owns them. None of this is true for copyrights. Copyright applications can be filed for a mere pittance. Further, the masses of cheaply copyright registered material are purportedly protected virtually forever with no maintenance fees required. (Lifetime plus seventy years or more at last count.) They need not be registered in each country wherein protection is purported to exist.

On top of that, works to be copyrighted can be "bundled" *ad infinitem*. Hence, if a songwriter or photographer has hundreds or thousands of works (songs or pictures) to copyright, he can staple them together in a single volume or load them all into a single digital file and cover them all under a single application with a single meager fee. The Patent and Trademark Office does not permit such

147

antics. There is no such "bundling" permitted in patent and trademark applications.

Finally, the present copyright system, which purports to preserve creator's rights essentially forever, does not preserve records of ownership to which anyone can easily refer. Copyright rules do not even always require that all the authors or composers be listed in any given registration. This has effectively "orphaned" many, many copyrights. That is to say, it has generated a tangle of rights wherein no one knows, without complex and expensive research, who owns which copyrighted works, nor or whether they are still under copyright protection.

This cheap, essentially perpetual, but ineffective, copyright system is not sustainable. It is far out of sync with the rest of our programs that DO work. We do, indeed, have a harmonization problem, but our problem is *internal*. Our copyright statutes are not in harmony with the rest of our IP system. As a result the Copyright Office is suffering financially. This is a losing proposition for all of us.

The fix is simple. First, we need to require US registration for copyrights under US protection. And, we need to establish maintenance fees for copyrights, just like everybody else pays for all other registered IP. Every few years, for as long as the Copyright Office preserves a copyright, the office needs to receive a fee for doing so. This is hardly unreasonable. It is, in fact, the norm for all intellectual property *except* copyrights.

If they are not maintained, this fact would be easily identified and the works would revert to the public domain. As a result of this clear reversion, some creations that likely would otherwise, have faded to eternal obscurity due to arbitrary legal obstacles might be revived to benefit the fame and purses of their creators.

Secondly, the number of separate works that can be covered under one copyright should be limited. It is reasonable to register a single copyright on a single novel of a thousand pages. It is absurd to supposedly cover an entire volume of individual songs, illustrations, photographs, or an entire digital video disc (DVD) of recordings under a single registration and fee. Such shotgun registrations as this make the contained intellectual property, although purportedly protected, virtually unidentifiable and unfindable.

This needs fixing. Individual works should be individually identified and individually registered. Their copyright registrations should be individually maintained with commensurate, periodic maintenance fees, just like patents and trademarks.

Simple, isn't it?

Now this may not be in harmony with the rest of the world, but frankly, harmonious homogeneity for its own sake has never been a means of progress, as much as we law practitioners would like it to be otherwise. All our "uniform legal codes" notwithstanding, it is *not* homogeneity that generates beneficial change nor any sort of change at all.[6]

On the other hand, such a system as I here propose would potentially foster great progress in the copyright world, while not necessarily pushing aside the present generous copyright terms or rights structure. It would simply render our system more functional and sustainable.

An example of the improved functionality that would result can be seen in the "orphaned works" problem mentioned above. Under the present system, when authors die, change address, or fail to follow statutory procedures, copyright ownership, successions, and estates easily become lost in antiquity. As a result, an unidentifiable (but probably huge) number of works may be free to enter the public domain, but nobody knows which they are. So, people are afraid to use them out of fear of copyright infringement suits. Vast realms of recorded music have been caught in this mire.

Thanks to our tangled and overbearing copyright statutes many unknown artists can rest assured that they will *remain* unknown forever.

Under such circumstances, the copyright system is functioning to precisely impede the very purpose for which it was created, which was to "encourage advancements in the useful arts." It was to do this by "establishing *for a limited time*" authors sole rights to the given works. In exchange for this protection, after that limited time expired those works would be available to all. However, as the copyright system exists at present, many works are kept from public exposure essentially forever due to the previously mentioned litigation fears. This causes the works to simply die in obscurity with little or no hope of resuscitation.

To those who have lobbied us into this short sighted system, it probably looked like a good idea at the time. In fact, it looked like a lifetime gravy train for a few record labels or publishers who could afford the necessary hype. But for most of our artists and their admirers, the old record label recording contract system and its control of music through unending copyright has been a losing proposition and continues to get worse. Witness the recent wholesale shift of bands and other recording artists to direct Internet distribution, bypassing the labels entirely.

In recognition of this obvious failure in statutory social engineering, our well-meaning legislators have created more legislation to deal with the orphaned works problem. The resulting quagmire made the whole copyright mess more complex and expensive without actually contributing to its support or success. The author has discussed this matter with one purported owner of a supposedly vast catalog of music who freely confided that he really has no idea what or how much he really owns. He is afraid to ask or even to look too closely. His business is forced to run more on bravado than on certainty of his assets.

A simple system of registration for individual works coupled with periodic maintenance fees for each would clear all this up. And it would be no great imposition. For works that are actively generating revenue, US registration and a periodic maintenance fee would be no big deal. When a work no longer generates income, maintenance fees would sensibly cease, the copyright would expire, and the work would be clearly on record as having reverted to the public domain. No questions as to the viability or ownership of the copyright would arise. They would be a matter of concise public record.

This is almost laughably elementary and obviously workable having been long successfully used for both patents and for trademarks, each of which is of vastly greater economic impact than copyrights. (See footnote 4, above.) We need to restructure our copyright system in such a way as to make it perform according to its purpose. Such a plan would cost less than the present one and would actually *function* in the bargain.

So it is indeed time to harmonize. But we are foolish to put America at greater economic disadvantage by trying to harmonize with an already discordant international community, using a failing system. Better that we seek, instead, consistency within our own system in such a way as to show the rest of the world how it should be done. Such common sense innovation is, after all, the traditional function that we fulfill here in America.

%%%%%%%%%%%%%%%%%%%%%%%%%%%%%%%%%%%%%
FOOTNOTES

[1] Performance Rights Act, S. 379 & H.R. 848

[2] "...despite China's size and relative economic strength during the world's downturn, the country's media market is

disproportionately small. For instance, the country's film administration estimates that a 100 million strong movie-going public generated total box office revenue of 3.3 billion yuan ($500 million) in 2007 - a tiny sliver of the US box office take." REUTERS, Wed 2 Dec 2009 / 11:59 EST, **http://www.reuters.com/ article/rbssMediaDiversified/idUSN1430884220090814?page Number=2&virtualBrandChannel=0**]

For an illustrative graphic representation of this market, also see: *Why are there so many/ so few USA based charts, 02-Dec-09* **http://tsort.info/music/faq_chart_count.htm**

[3] This potential income is not, in fact particularly significant. Entertainment industry hype might lead some to believe that showbiz is a big money proposition, but it is not. It makes only a few (very few) privileged folks somewhat wealthy. However, if we peruse the top ten US exports, we find that music, movies, and videos are nowhere on the chart. In fact, in 2007, number ten on the list was "computer accessories at $29.4 billion. In comparison, DVD tapes and discs came in at a paltry 1/6th of that ($4.9 billion). *Top American Exports in 2007 Leading USA Products Include Semiconductors and Civilian Aircraft* © Daniel Workman July 27, 2008 **http://import-export.suite101.com/article.cfm/top_ american_exports_in_2007#ixzz0YYy6VbJb**

In the following year's report (2008) DVDs, tapes, and discs did not even merit mention. *America's Top Imports & Exports 2008, US Shows Trade Advantages in Civilian Aircraft and Semiconductors,* © Daniel Workman, Oct 6, 2009, **http://import-export.suite101.com/article.cfm/americas_top_imports_exports_ 2008#ixzz0YZ1Rq0Ip**

[4] Business 101: *"Money come in--good. Money go out-- bad."* (I already told you this was not rocket science.)

[5] The patent examination backlog is, admittedly, increasing, but until relatively recently the Patent Office, although earning enough to pay its own way, had its funds regularly raided by Congress to pay for other less financially sound programs. The USPTO has earned a far greater harvest than they have been allowed to reap. Now, with miraculously bad timing, although the Patent Office is now allowed to keep more of their harvest, the harvest has due to the economic downturn become suddenly skimpy. And under new patent reform legislation, things will get much worse.

[6] For example, it is not homogeneity, that preserved the Common Law or made it great, but the lack thereof. The rather *unharmonious* Norman Invasion, the American Revolution, and the fifty separate, but sovereign, members of the United States have all contributed to the sustained vitality and continued relevance of our Common Law.

Now Common Law concepts are being quietly and sensibly absorbed even into European Union Law (although under different titles and without attribution). The comparatively recent EU doctrine of "acte éclairé" is an important example. European courts, being Civil Law domains, theoretically do not brook the Common Law doctrine of *precedent*. In fact, they are rather proud of such foolishness.

But *acte éclairé* dictates that issues similar to matters previously decided should not be referred for decision again. Instead, the same result should be applied. This is essentially the doctrine of *precedent* under a different name.

(With the exception of your British shipmates do not mention this to any European Union pals, especially not the French. It will only make them grumpy.)

153

# PATENT REFORM ACT
# ADDENDUM

In view of recent legislation emanating from points east, we are moved to add a late update on patent law. This new legislation is generally known as The Patent Reform Act and is another installment in our continuing saga of "international harmonization." The Patent Reform Act of 2011 was signed into law by President Obama on 16 Sept 2011.

## KEY PROVISIONS

### ☠ First to File

**This Act shifts the US from a "first to invent" system to a "first to file"** system as is used in the rest of the world. This is a big, BIG change. It moves the focus from inventing to patent filing. It awards patent rights to the first to file a patent application no matter who invented first. Previously, US patent rights belonged to the first person to actually invent any given gadget, even if the inventor "lost the race to the Patent Office" (within limits).

To make this compatible with the rest of the world's inferior systems, **inventors who let their inventions be known prior to filing patent applications lose the rights to seek patents at all.** However, during transition, the Act provides a **one year grace period** for certain disclosures by the inventor, prior to patent application. It leaves some questions as to what the circumstances of the disclosure may be. Refer to the previous chapter, "Mum's the Word."

### ☠ Assignment

If an inventor is obligated to assign the rights to his invention to somebody else, but cannot or has refused to do so the **rightful assignee may submit a substitute statement of assignment.**[1]

### ☠ Defense to Infringement Based on Prior Use

You can defend against charges of infringement by proving you used the invention at least a year prior to the patentee's patent application. This defense cannot be applied, however, against university inventions.

### ☠ Third Party Challenges to Patents

The Act creates three new and expanded methods that a third party can use to challenge a patent. ("Third party" = "Not the patent holder or the Patent Office.")

### ☠ Pre-Issuance Third Party Submissions

Anybody (any "third party") may submit opposition to any pending patent application.

### ☠ Third Party Requested Post Grant Review

This is similar to previous "reexamination" provisions. It provides a special procedure for demanding a "second look" at recently granted patents. This must be requested (if at all) within one year from grant of the patent. The patent holder may not participate in the review.

## ☠ *Inter Partes* Post-Grant Review

This is a reexamination requested by a third party, but in resolution of which, the patent holder gets to participate, not just the Patent Office and the third party challenger. (That is where the term *inter partes* comes in. Lawyers demand *some* Latin, even patent attorneys. It is a compulsion, so we humor them.)

## ☠ Supplemental Reexamination

At the patent owner's request the Patent Office may consider, reconsider, and correct information in a granted patent.

## ☠ Jurisdiction and Procedure

❀ The **Board of Patent Appeals and Interferences is replaced by the Patent Trial and Appeal Board,** having substantially the same duties but with new and expanded procedures. From there, appeals go directly to the US Court of Appeals for the Federal Circuit, bypassing federal district courts.

❀ The **Court of Appeals for the Federal Circuit gets exclusive jurisdiction over patent appeals.** This is on the whole a good thing.[2]

❀ It **dictates that all patent or copyright civil litigation is subject to removal to the local federal district court.**[3]

❀ It allows *joinder* (joining up in a single case) of

accused patent infringers into one action as defendants *only* if the right to relief "arises to the same offending transaction or series of transactions." [4]

❀ It **gives a particular Law Firm (and their client) a "pass" on their mishandling of a particular patent application.** A certain large law firm missed a deadline and got sued on a large scale for malpractice. This bill retroactively lets them off for dropping the ball. [5]

## ☠ Fees and Fee Setting

The Act **gives the Patent Office independent authority to set and adjust fees. But it leaves Congress with freedom to commandeer the fees** instead of leaving them to support the Patent Office. [6]

It introduces an incentive to file electronically (a **new $400 supplemental fee on applications that are filed on paper**).

It **creates a new classification of applicant, termed "micro entity,"** entitled to a **seventy-five percent reduction in specified fees.** A "micro entity" is defined as an applicant who:

- ❀ qualifies as a small entity (most small businesses),
- ❀ has not been named as the inventor in more than four previous patent applications,
  *and*
- ❀ has a gross income below a certain designated level
  *or*
- ❀ is a university or employee thereof.

## ☠ Best Mode

Historically, inventors must, at peril of having their patents invalidated, disclose the best version or *mode* of the claimed invention. The Act maintains this requirement for the inventor to disclose the best mode. But **failure to disclose the best mode is no longer grounds for patent claim cancelation nor for patent invalidation.**

## ☠ Patent Markings

For devices that are "patent pending," are "patented," or were previously patented, the Act **allows "virtual markings."** (Virtual markings are markings that direct the public to an Internet site where patent information may be found regarding the article in question.)

This unknots the huge tangle created by previous legislation penalizing "false markings." It essentially backs off from the legislatively created "false marking" disaster that set patent marking "trolls" on the prowl suing in all directions for inaccurate or out of date patent markings. This is good.

## ☠ Financial Business Methods

It eliminates financial and tax tactical manipulation software as patentable subject matter. (This prohibition does not apply against mere tax form preparation or accounting software.) [7]

☠ **Failure to Obtain Advice of Counsel**
**as grounds for finding willful infringement**

Failure to obtain opinion of counsel **may not be used to prove that any infringement was willful or induced.** This provides much needed clarification of a matter about which the courts could not agree.

## SUMMARY

**The supposed purpose of the Patent Reform Act is to "harmonize" our system** with other patent systems around the world. Most of the world uses a "first to file" system, which is easier to administer. The United States has always used a "first to invent system" that emphasizes creative production. So through some twisted logic, the contention is that the US system needs fixing. It needs "harmonization." But **this Act does not "harmonize."** All it really does is make the Patent System administratively more simple. This raises the question as to which is more important, administrative convenience or effectiveness.

The US patent system has long been the most productive patent system in the world. It has succeeded beyond anybody's wildest dreams. It is the bulwark of our wealth. It undeniably has some problems, but **our biggest problems with it date back to emergence of US "Business Method Patents" in the 1990's.** Virtually all Business Method Patents are for computer programs. Opening the field to allow patents for software seemed like a good idea at the time. Instead, it became our biggest patent headache.

In hindsight we appear to have made a stupendous and expensive mistake. It has resulted in massive patent examination backlogs and multiple patents issuing for practically the same inventions essentially simultaneously on a continuous basis. We now have vast numbers of ongoing patent suits, and huge patent portfolios constantly bought, sold, litigated, overlapped, and infringed by Google®, Microsoft®, Nokia®, Apple®, and a number of non-producing patent-holding companies ("patent trolls").

The patent system simply does not well serve intangible inventions. The attempt to make it do so has created a litigation firestorm and an extremely hostile environment for entrepreneurs and startups. (Things have gotten so bad that, even lawyers who stand to make a bundle on this mess, concede that it was a super blooper.)

The rest of the world already decided that computer program patents are not a good idea, and, generally speaking, *the rest of the world does not permit them.* In this, we are, indeed, out of harmony. If we really set out to "harmonize," with the rest of the world, our legislature would recognize this and *undo the mistake.* Instead, they just shoveled legislation around it. The Act does not address the problem.

**Succinctly putting this all together, our biggest patent problems will continue. The litigation firestorms will continue to rage. Small startups will continue to be sued into oblivion, and small inventors are abandoned with even greater disadvantages than they had before.[8]** Unfortunately, such startups and entrepreneurs comprise our primary sources of new employment. Therefore, this act promises to have generally the same effect on job creation as King Herod had on the Bethlehem Playground Association.

%%%%%%%%%%%%%%%%%%%%%%%%%%%%%%%%%%%%%%%

## ADDENDUM FOOTNOTES

[1] This is important to universities, especially, who have recently learned that their obligatory patent assignment agreements do not hold water particularly well. See <u>Stanford v Roche 2008-1509, -1510 (Fed. Cir. Sept. 30, 2009)</u>.

[2] This shuts out federal district court judges who mostly majored in, to name a few, English, social anthropology, and afternoon keggers, thereby achieving questionable background for occasionally addressing technological innovations. Consistently giving patent cases to the same court at least guarantees that the judges concerned get some experience in dealing with reality on a regular basis. This has long been the predominant custom anyway.

[3] This moves litigation farther out of reach for the small operator. It ensures greater difficulty for presumptuous smalltime lawyers out in the hinterlands who have been known to run to local courts and jam up the tracks of sleazebag Washington law firm bulldozers and their stinky porno-pushing copyright clients. (No bias here!)

[4] This provision is precisely what the copyright system needs to put a lid on the "sleazebag Washington law firm bulldozers and their stinky porno copyright clients," addressed above. But unfortunately, this provision does not encompass copyright matters. It only applies to patents. So abusive movie copyright litigation joining thousands of defendants into single suits on the most flimsy of evidence remains festering in the courts.

161

[5] So much for preserving any credibility for the Act or its legislators. If you happen to miss a deadline, try buying legislation like this for yourself sometime, and let me know how you get on.

[6] Essentially, Congress abdicated its responsibility for setting fees, but retained the power to confiscate them. This confiscation has, historically, been a problem for the Patent Office. Fees cannot be set to dependably defray expenses unless the Patent Office can know how much of the fees they will get to keep. So the central problem remains.

[7] This is good. So far, observing Wall Street financial management *á' la* disastrous computer automated decision making, their patent applications look like "going to Hell in a hand basket," while seeking a patent monopoly on the hand basket.

[8] Forgive our reticent manner. The term *firestorm* is merely a polite substitute for a salty seaman's description of a storm using the same number of letters but more odiferous expectations.

# Appendix I

# The Catechism of Intellectual Property Crime

## A Compendium of Penalties for Imitation, the Sincerest Form of Flattery

(with contributions by Tracy Kane, Attorney at Law)

# Friar Tuck would love this part.

*Pirate's Rule #24:* "...ye shall know the truth and the truth shall make you free.[1]"

(But if the judge knows the truth, it may get you 20 years with no time off for good behavior.)

Now come we to the nitty-gritty criminal statutes of intellectual property. Not many folks are actually knowledgeable as to the specifics of intellectual property *crime*. It just does not fit in anybody's particular legal bailiwick. The mere name itself seems a bit skewed. Further, this realm seems to constantly encompass ever broader territory. It appears to cross pollinate with "cybercrime" and "identification theft," for example. Bluntly said, "intellectual property crime" is vague, wooly, and comfortably accommodated in no clearly defined area of law; An unwanted stepchild.

However, we must address it, for the existence of criminal IP statutes unquestionably leaves some nagging questions in the minds of the general public; Particularly music fans; Particularly music fans who are a bit uncomfortable when contemplating the possibility of earning jail time whilst in pursuit of their listening pleasure. This section equips the casual reader with general guidance and points him to locations containing more detail for answering these questions.

Be mindful that this addresses only US federal statutes. The individual states also have their own specialized collections of legislative mandates on the same subjects. Be also aware that the legislative juggernaut never rests. So, we cannot swear this compendium to be complete. Frankly, things have gotten so out of hand that *nobody* can keep track of all the federal criminal statutes, rules, or regulations, and no exhaustive collection of them exists. Shucks, nobody can even count them, though by my favorite cutlass, many have gone near bowlegged and blind in the attempt.[2]

We gently open with a small appetizer statute, an introduction to genuine, counterfeiting and forgery. It addresses *copying*, although strictly speaking, it is not normally considered an intellectual property offense. The subject is do-it-yourself private production of fake money (as opposed to legally acceptable government production of fake money). We offer this as a comparative baseline statutory sample; Something against which we can compare all that follows.

As you may discern from the next lecturer's lingo, he is not a pirate of the open seas, but a river predator known by lowly titles like *scuffle hunter, night plunderer, copeman* or *wrecker.*" This shallow waterman details for us the risks of meddling in copyrights, the most simple, most common, and often the most shallow and frivolous of all intellectual properties. He also gives a peek at trademark and trade secret criminal statutes and laws.

Comments and introductory notes for each statute appear in **this bold font for the reader's convenience.** The statutes themselves are *italicized.* [3]

%%%%%%%%%%%%%%%%%%%%%%%%%%%%%%%%%%%%%
FOOTNOTES

[1] John 8:32, Authorized Version

[2] The last documented attempt to count the federal criminal "laws" was by the American Bar Association in 1998. They gave up the task in defeat without producing a specific estimate. (See *Wall Street Journal*, "Many Failed Efforts to Count Nation's Federal Laws", Sat/Sun July 23-24, 2011, pg. A10.) Subsequently, things have become even more confused than they were then.

[3] Technical note: For the purposes of the following explanations, the terms *jail, brig, slammer, hoosegow, clink, can, lockup, cooler, chain locker, big house, up the river,* and *publicly funded low security residential recreational facility popularly frequented by Illinois legislators*, are considered interchangeable.

# Intellectual Property Crime Catechism
## Lesson #1

# Counterfeiting for Fun and Profit

*Pirate's rule #25: If counterfeiting is your game, don't fake trademarks or copyrights. Print money. It's safer.*

**Following is the key federal counterfeiting and forgery statute. Note the beautiful brevity. Note the significant penalties. This is what the law against genuine counterfeiting of actual US dollars looks like. Keep the simplicity of these statutes in mind as we next set out to explore the worlds of copyright and trademark infringement ("counterfeiting") statutes.**

# COUNTERFEITING AND FORGERY
## 18 USC § 471

*Whoever, with intent to defraud, falsely makes, forges, counterfeits, or alters any obligation or other security of the United States, shall be fined under this title or imprisoned not more than 20 years, or both.*

END OF STATUTE

The key thing to note other than the simplicity is that the specified penalty comprises many years in the slammer. Specifically, the assigned jail time is *twenty years for counterfeiting actual US money.* Mark that fact and hold it in your mind for later comparison as we review other statutes wherein we find that this penalty is no greater than the penalty for "counterfeiting" considerably more frivolous stuff.

If "brevity," is indeed, "the soul of wit," the above precise pieces of legislative prose must be quite witty. But this is the last we shall see of such concise wit or wisdom for this is the point of departure for our tour of intellectual property crimes. You may not find our statutes particularly witty, wise, or even realistic.

Such matters are a good and proper fit as issues for civil litigation, but they get pounded into criminal court slots only with significant discomfort. This is because the named offenses can, in practice, be in gray areas difficult to define or discern. So rather than simply trying to determine "who done it" (or "didn't") the courts are left trying to first decide whether anybody committed any crime in the first place.

There is no excuse for this situation. Our legislators (bless their lobbied little hearts) created it by their continued compulsion to throw every matter to into criminal courts whether it belongs there or not, thereby creating crimes where none previously existed or could have been guessed.

The next statute promptly initiates a novel statutory use for the word "counterfeit," clearly indicating that the word no longer applies merely to imitation money. Admittedly, the proper term "trademark infringement" is rather ho-hum. So in a grand gesture of showmanship, we dramatically convert it to *counterfeiting* or better yet, to *piracy*, thereby pushing aside boring old fuddy-duddy concepts like "false advertising," and "truth in packaging."

The expressions *counterfeiting* and *piracy* elicit much more entertaining images of Scar Faced Al, or maybe Blackbeard and are after all much more fun to legislate about...totally without credibility, but much more fun.

**Note the below penalties of up to *fifteen million smackers and twenty years.* strongly resembling the penalties assessed for real counterfeiting of real money.**

## <u>TRAFFICKING IN COUNTERFEIT GOODS OR SERVICES</u>
## <u>18 USC. § 2320</u>

*OFFENSE:*

    *To traffic (or attempt to traffic) in goods or services, labels, wrappers, stickers, badges, emblems, medallions, charms, tags, monikers, cattle brands, tattoos, funny hats, custom ornamental dental grills, packaging, or documentation, knowingly using a* **counterfeit mark***, likely to confuse or deceive:*

*PENALTY, FIRST OFFENSE:*

    ☠ *By an individual: Fine up to $2 million clams and/or up to* **10 years** *in the slammer.*

    ☠ *By other than an individual (corporation, company, Mongol horde...): Fine up to $5 million smackers.*

*PENALTY, SUBSEQUENT OFFENSE(S):*

    ☠ *By an individual: Fine up to $5 million and/or up to* **20 years** *government sponsored vacation.*

    ☠ *By other than an individual: Fine up to $15 million.*

**Yup, ya' read that right, pilgrim. A solitary malefactor gets twenty years, just like for real counterfeiting of real money.**

*plus....*

☠ **DESTRUCTION** *of any article bearing or consisting of a counterfeit mark and any of property used to commit or to facilitate the violation.*

☠ **FORFEITURE** *of any property constituting or derived from any proceeds obtained, directly or indirectly, by the offense. (Generally governed by procedures in section 413 of the Comprehensive Drug Abuse Prevention and Control Act (21 USC. § 853). This is pretty broad and peremptory stuff.*

☠ **RESTITUTION** *to victims.*

☠ **A VICTIM IMPACT STATEMENT** *may be submitted in evidence. (The offer of an alternative penalty, namely, compelling the offender to French kiss a catfish, was defeated in committee.)*

*LEGAL TIP: All defenses, affirmative defenses, limitations on remedies applicable in an action under the Lanham Act (i.e. "good old trademark law") or other legal hocus pocus are also available here.*

*LEGAL TIP: "Counterfeit mark" means essentially **identical** (not merely similar) to a mark registered in the United States Patent and Trademark Office (and in use whether or not the defendant knew). "Counterfeit goods" follow the same simple rule of resemblance. But for some reason, design patent infringement is not included under this rule. (If it seems that patents and all the other really serious IP stuff get short changed in this, it is easy to explain. More frivolous entertainers than serious engineers serve in Congress.)*

*LEGAL TIP:* *"Financial gain" (as opposed to "economic advantage," apparently) is defined in this act. It "includes the receipt, or expected receipt, of anything of value." Remember this definition for "financial gain". It means any sort of benefit from your underhanded malefactions. According to federal sentencing guidelines, "commercial advantage" or "financial gain" can merely mean trading music files.[1]*

## *Intellectual Property Crime Catechism*
### *Question #1*

## *Question: Can we go to jail for trademark infringement?*

## *Answer: YES WE CAN! YES WE CAN! (But, only if we do a really professional job.)*

%%%%%%%%%%%%%%%%%%%%%%%%%%%%%%%%%%%%%%%%%
FOOTNOTE

[1] *2004 Federal Sentencing Guidelines Manual 2B5.3. Criminal Infringement of Copyright or Trademark.* As with federal IP statutes, these guidelines are subject to amendment and continue to be revised. For example, in October 2005, the US Sentencing

Commission issued new amendments to the Guideline's provisions particularly applicable to intellectual property offenses. See *2005 Amendments to the US Sentencing Guidelines for IP Offenses* (October 2005) and *2000 Amendments to Sentencing Guidelines for IP Offenses* (May 2000). Also see: **http://www.justice.gov/criminal/cybercrime/iplaws.html** .

# *Intellectual Property Crime Catechism*
## *Lesson #2*

# *Corporate Espionage*

*Pirate's Rule #26: Corporate espionage is not just clever competition. It is a crime.*

Next we address trade secrets. US trade secret matters have, historically, been overseen by the separate US states and fell under civil not criminal law. But federal legislators, subject as they are to legislative obsessive-compulsive disorder, noticed this area in which they previously had not meddled. As a result, we now have federal criminal trade secret offenses. And individual US states have also commenced creation of their own criminal trade secret statutes.

# THEFT OF TRADE SECRETS AND ECONOMIC ESPIONAGE
## 18 USC. § 1832

**OFFENSE:**

*Any **mangy skunk** who, in some sneakin'-big-city Wall-Street-style-shenanigans, with intent to **heist a trade secret** that is related to or included in a product in interstate or foreign commerce;*

❀ *Makes off with the skinny;*

*or*

❀ *Copies, duplicates, sketches, draws, photographs, downloads, uploads, alters, destroys, photocopies, replicates, transmits, delivers, sends, mails, communicates, conveys, looks sideways at, or tattoos it on his bosun's backside;*

*or*

❀ *Receives, buys, bootlegs, or possesses such information, knowing it was light fingered;*

*or*

❀ *Even attempts any of these low down rotten stunts;*

*or*

❀ *Conspires with some other weasel to commit any of them egg-sucking offenses, then he gits;*

**PENALTIES:**

☠ *Invitation to break rocks for up to **10 years**, **fined**, or both,*

*except as provided in the subsection below, which says;*

☠ *That also goes for the herd he rode in with, cuz **any organization** (who'd probably also steal the straw from their mother's kennel) that commits them shenanigans will be hit up for as much as **$5,000,000,** or, what the heck, even **$10,000,000**.*

175

☠ *And furthermore, as fer the polecat who, intending or* **knowing that it will benefit any foreign** *government, instrumentality, or agent, pulls any of them same mangy skunk tricks (See also 18 USC. § 1831.), he'll git his scrawny butt fined up to* **$500,000** *or jailed up to* **15 years***, or both.*

## *Intellectual Property Crime Catechism*

## *Question #2*

# Question: Can we go to jail just for sneakin' a peek at Colonel Sander's secret recipe?

# Answer: YES WE CAN! YES WE CAN!

# Intellectual Property Crime Catechism
## Lesson #3

# Sneak Video Recordings
## (of live performances)

Pirate's Rule# 27: Fools sneak
recordings from theaters.
(But, there is a special berth in the Hell
bound ship for people who text during
performances.)

This statute criminalizes making sneak recordings of live musical performances. Check out the bonus. The offended recording artists or movie stars can come to testify at your sentencing! You could get your own personal victim impact statement from your own favorite star!

## FIXATION OF AND UNAUTHORIZED TRAFFICKING IN SOUND RECORDINGS AND MUSIC VIDEOS OF LIVE MUSICAL PERFORMANCES
### 18 USC. § 2319A

*OFFENSE:*

*For any nerdy, techno-dweeb, who for commercial advantage or financial gain, (and what isn't?);*

☠ *Makes sneak recordings, or reproductions of sounds, or sounds and images [but note, not silent images] of a live musical performance;*

*or*

☠ *Makes them public;*

*or*

☠ *Traffics in, distributes, sells, rents, fences, hawks, hucksters, or peddles off the back of a truck, such recordings (or offers to do so even outside the US).*

*PENALTIES, FIRST OFFENSE:*

☠ *Hoosegow: **up to 5 years;** and/or*

☠ ***Monetary fine.***

*PENALTY, SUBSEQUENT OFFENSE(S):*

☠ *More Hoosegow: **up to 10 years;** and/or*

☠ ***Monetary fine.***

*and, in any case,*

☠ ***DESTRUCTION** of the recordings, and any associated plates, molds, matrices, masters, tapes, film negatives, scrimshaw, cave paintings, or native American style sand art, and optionally, of any gear used for reproducing such recordings.*

*BUT WAIT, THERE'S MORE!*
☠ *Seizure and Forfeiture of the goods, if fixed outside of the United States (just like customs contraband);*
*plus*
☠ *As an added bonus, for this limited offer, your favorite judicial bureaucrat gets to hobnob with your own favorite music artist to get a victim impact statement.*

*LEGAL TIP: So far as we can tell, it is not a defense to assert that the performance was not in fact melodic. Apparently, any attempt or claim to be musical is considered sufficient to complete the offense....er... sorry, we meant "to constitute a musical performance."*

# More Sneak Video
# Recordings
## (from movie houses)

**The following statute is of essentially the same nature as stuff in the previous statute, except it is for movie performances, not live musical appearances. It targets the folks who sneak all those really bad, low quality, off angle, videos of new movies before they are released on DVD. (What we REALLY need is jail time for the jerks who TALK and TEXT during performances; Just one river man's opinion.)**

# UNAUTHORIZED RECORDING OF MOTION PICTURES IN A MOTION PICTURE EXHIBITION FACILITY
## 18 USC. § 2319B

**OFFENSE:**

Any technologically challenged, but compulsive home movie addict who gets nailed because he (or she, though, we all know it's pretty much always a "he")...uses a video recorder to **record or transmit a copy of movie from/in a theater show** (or attempts to);

**PENALTY, FIRST OFFENSE:**

Low security recreational facility: **up to 3 years and/or fine;**

**PENALTY, SUBSEQUENT OFFENSE(S);**

More low security recreation: **up to 6 years and/fine;**

**plus, in either case**

☠ **FORFEITURE AND DESTRUCTION** of all unauthorized copies and any equipment used in connection with the offense;
   and
☠ **VICTIM IMPACT STATEMENT:** During the preparation of the presentence report, yak-y-dee-yak, under rule 32(c) of the Federal Rules of Criminal Procedure, blah, blah, victims shall yada, yada a victim impact statement...[Kowtowing to silly egos of clueless, but privileged movie stars and self-important moguls, this section blithers on for several more paragraphs].

**LEGAL TIP:** If you are incompetent enough to get caught offendin' this statute more than once, you can also draw **six years** in the big house.[1]

180

*LEGAL TIP: IMMUNITY FOR THEATER OPERATORS:* The operator of a movie theater may [if he thinks he's man enough] shackle, shanghai, or otherwise detain any person suspected of this offense, "for the purpose of questioning or summoning" a cop [Although, paraphrasing Groucho Marks, "Why he'd want to question a cop, I can't imagine!"]

*LEGAL TIP:* Take heed, your video capable iPhone® can be used as evidence against you if you carry it into a theater.

## *Intellectual Property Crime Catechism*

### *Question #3:*

## Question: Can we go to jail just for sneaking video recordings while in a theater?

## Answer: YES WE CAN! YES WE CAN!

%%%%%%%%%%%%%%%%%%%%%%%%%%%%%%%%%%%%%%%%%

FOOTNOTE

[1] *This creates a painful situation to imagine. A couple of huge, scarred-up thugs sidle up to you in the prison exercise yard, and ask, "Whadaya in for?" Do you admit that you were caught sneaking a movie camera into a kiddy matinee, or do you preserve your dignity and claim to be a serial killer? Tough decision.*

181

# Intellectual Property Crime Catechism
## Lesson #4
# The "Do As I Say, Not As I Do" Statutes
### (Wire Taps)

*Pirate's Rule #28: If you want to learn real pirate skills, work for the government.*

This lesson is a loooooong one. It sallies forth into the land of "*They can, but you can't.*" Why can't you? Because "they" said so. In this land are practiced a number of dark arts that Uncle Sam has perfected for decades.

These fall under the heading, "communications interception." A couple of these statutes apparently set out to corral, among other things, the "unofficial" Cable Guy and the dude selling hot cell phones out of the back of his van.

They criminalize "counterfeit access devices." that get you into phone or cable TV systems. We are not sure what "counterfeit access" is. All the ones we've seen give you "real access," illegal or not.

They also by the way, appear to especially criminalize snookering credit card payments out of unwary users by using their illegal access device.

Noting that these statutes list penalties for the illegal access offenses, look closely, for there's that *twenty year prison term*, again. Just like real counterfeiting. Is it becoming clear why they shoehorn the word "counterfeit" into the statutes? If you give it a serious name, you can assign serious jail time with a straight face. They can lay on penalties that are just like those given to true printers of fake money.

Mere possession of a qualifying radio receiver can get you locked away for up to *five years*. Now, as in baseball, we can only call'em the way we see 'em. And the way we see this one, it sure looks like calling Michael Jackson a shortstop just because he wore a glove.

In contrast, although *real* bootleggin' of real white-lightnin' continues to be illegal, nobody gets jailed just for having a fine thirty gallon still with a copper bottomed distilling pot, water cooled worm, automatic temperature controlled gas heater, porcelain slobber pot, oak thumper, and special custom reflux-flow neck...not that we know anybody who has such a thing. So, why the big deal?

The answer is that history simply cannot resist repeating itself. Uncle Sam has initiated thousands of eager techno-dweebs into the dark arts of communications interception, and now he's paying the price. And it hurts.

In analogy, a few centuries ago, Queen Elizabeth the First ("Gawd bless 'er!") trained up quite a mob of "privateers" (government sponsored pirates) in her service. Francis Drake led the examples. This came back to bite her in the stern sheets when privateering work got scarce. Good Queen Lizzy ("Gawd bless 'er!") ended up with skilled pirates stalking her own ships. Now, the same thing is happening to Uncle Sam with his trained intercept operators. And like 'er Majesty (Gawd bless 'er) he is going apoplectic over it.

## FRAUD AND RELATED ACTIVITY IN CONNECTION WITH ACCESS DEVICES
### 18 USC. § 1029

*OFFENSE:*

*Them what with low down, no-better-than-a carpet-baggin'-Yankee intentions (a.k.a. "knowingly and with fraudulent intent");*

☠ *Uses or traffics in* **counterfeit access devices;**
*or worse*
☠ *Uses or traffics in unauthorized access devices* **during any one year period**, *and thereby gains greater than or equal to* **$1,000 value;**

☠ *Possesses **fifteen or more** counterfeit or unauthorized access devices;*
*or*
☠ *Produces, traffics in, has control or custody of, or **possesses device-making equipment**;*
*or*
☠ ***Effects transactions**, with an access device issued to another person, in order to receive payment of $1,000 or more;*
*or*
☠ ***Solicits** anybody to: offer an access device; or sell information about, or to obtain, an access device;*
*or*
☠ *Uses, produces, traffics in, controls, or possesses a **telecom instrument** that has been modified or altered to obtain unauthorized use of telecom services;*
*or*
☠ *Uses, produces, traffics in, controls or possesses a **scanning receiver (ANY scanner? This may be one of them laws we just politely ignore so as not to embarrass our honored legislators.)**;*
*or*
☠ *Uses, produces, traffics in, controls, or **possesses hardware or software, to modify identity of a telecom instrument** so that it may be used to obtain unauthorized telecom service;*
*or*
☠ *Without the authorization of the **credit card** system member, arranges for another person to present to the member, for payment, records of transactions made by an access device:*
*can git;*

## PENALTIES, FIRST OFFENSE:
☠ *For some offenses, up to **10 years** in the chain locker;*

*and/or*
☠  *Monetary fine.*

☠  *For some other offenses under this title, incarceration may extend up to **15 years**. (You'll need to look up the details.)*

**PENALTY, SUBSEQUENT OFFENSES**:
☠  *Up to **20 years** and/or **fine** (per this title).*

**PENALTY IN ANY CASE:**
☠  **Forfeiture and seizure** *of anything within horizon range.*

**Fascinatin' ain't it?  We can hardly tear ourselves away, so continuing in this entertaining vein, we review awards for;**

## MANUFACTURE, DISTRIBUTION, POSSESSION AND ADVERTISING OF WIRE, ORAL OR ELECTRONIC COMMUNICATION INTERCEPTING DEVICES PROHIBITED 18 USC. § 2512

**OFFENSE:**
*ANYBODY ('cept the "Law", & phone companies, of course) who;*

☠  **Sends through the mail, or sends or carries** *in interstate or foreign commerce, any communications-tapping device;*
*or*

☠  **Manufactures, assembles, possesses, or sells** *any communications-tapping device;*
*or*

☠  *Places in any newspaper, magazine, handbill, or other publication [the "world-wide-Web" is too ultra-modern to get*

specifically included here?!] **any advertisement** of any communications-tapping device, or that promotes use of such device for the purpose communications-tapping;
    whilst
    ☠ Knowing or having reason to know that such advertisement will be sent through the mail or transported in interstate or foreign commerce;
    can git;

**PENALTY:**
Relegation to facilitating brief visual examinations of the interiors of recently broken rock strata extracts for a period of up to **5 years and/or fined** as provided for elsewhere in this title.

**Oh by the way, this general policy also applies to any other method of getting a free ride off the local cable provider as described in the next section...........**

# Snakin' a Cable

# Connection

## <u>UNAUTHORIZED INTERCEPTION OR RECEIPT,</u>
## <u>OR</u>
## <u>ASSISTANCE IN INTERCEPTING OR RECEIVING</u>
## <u>SERVICE</u>
## <u>47 USC. § 553</u>

**OFFENSE:**
DON'T, repeat, DON'T go and **intercept or receive, communications service over a cable system**, nor assist nobody in doing so 'les'n speeecifically authorized. No sort of service, whatsoever. Nothing, no how.

**LEGAL TIP:** Note that **"assist" includes manufacture or distribution of equipment** for unauthorized reception over a cable system. ["Cable" means "wideband cable" not "plain old telephone" ("POT") line.]

**PENALTIES, FIRST OFFENSE:**
☠ **FINE:** Up to **$1000;**
and/or
☠ up to **6 months** in the pokey;

☠ **EXCEPT:** Violation for commercial advantage or private financial gain gets hit up for up to **$50,000** and/or up to **2 years** in the pokey (first offense).

**PENALTIES, SUBSEQUENT OFFENSES:**
☠ fined up to **$100,000;**
and/or
☠ up to **5 years** pokified.

**LEGAL TIP:** Remember that each such device constitutes a separate offense.

**CIVIL ACTION REMEDIES AND COMPENSATION:**
☠ In civil action, a US district court, or other court of competent jurisdiction, **may award damages, full costs, and attorneys' fees**.

188

☠ *Aggrieved may recover actual damages and any profits, or statutory **damages of $250 to $10,000.***

☠ *If the violation was committed willfully and **for purposes of commercial advantage or private financial gain**, damages awarded, actual or statutory, may be **increased by up to $50,000** (and have a REAL nice day).*

*EXCEPTIONS: Where the courts find the doe eyed and obviously pure hearted violator was **not aware** and had no reason to believe the acts constituted violation (yeah, sure) **damages may be reduced to as low as $100.***

*LEGAL TIP: NO PREEMPTION OF STATE'S POWERS: Individual states also may enact their own freeloader statutes, it they are so foolish. (The trusting legislators of Tennessee, for example, recently got snookered into passing vague and misguided entertainment industry protection legislation, apparently without actually knowing what the lobby loiterers were selling them. Tennessee has made it illegal to share your "entertainment subscription," whatever that is.)[1]*

**The next two statutes, essentially more of the same from above, say in short, "WE BE NSA.[2] YOU NOT." That is to say that if the NSA does it, then you can't do it. (Union rules, we reckon?) Uncle Sam has a statutory monopoly on lowdown, underhanded eavesdropping. For "Do-It-Yourselfers," there are some stiff penalties.[1]**

189

# The Porthole Listenin',
# Eavesdroppin', Gossip
# Mongerin',
# Blabbermouth Statutes

## UNAUTHORIZED PUBLICATION OR USE OF COMMUNICATONS
## 47 USC. § 605

**OFFENSE:**

☠ *No eaves droppin' hombre,* **receiving, transmitting, or assisting in either, of any interstate or foreign communication** *by wire or radio shall go blabbin' or otherwise* **divulge its existence, and/or what it says** *or means, except through authorized channels of transmission or reception, and unless authorized by the sender, or except as authorized by Chapter 119, Title 18. (Now, ya'll git to figure out what is "authorized.")*

☠ *In fact, ya'll better not, unless entitled thereto, receive or* **assist in receiving any interstate or foreign radio comms and use 'em** *for your own benefit or for the benefit of any other skunk also not entitled thereto.*

☠ *No person having received any intercepted radio comms or having become acquainted with the contents shall go blabbin' about, or **divulge the existence, contents, or meaning, nor use 'em for his own benefit** or for the benefit of some other weasel not entitled neither.*

*PENALTIES:*
☠ *Up to **$100,000** and/or **5 years** in the can.*

*OFFENSE:*
☠ *Anybody who merely **manufactures, assembles, modifies, imports, exports, sells, or distributes any device** primarily of assistance in the unauthorized decryption (**"code bustin'"**) of satellite cable programming, or direct-to-home satellite services, or any other activity prohibited by this section gits;*

*PENALTIES:*
☠ *Fine of up to **$500,000**, and/or slammered up to **5 years**, for each violation;*
     *and/or*
☠ ***Civil Damages** of up to **$100,000 per** violation.*

*LEGAL TIP: These penalties are in addition to those prescribed under any other provision of this subchapter.*

*LEGAL TIP: Each device constitutes a separate violation.*

*EXCEPTIONS: Radio signals transmitted intentional-like to the **general public, or related to ships, aircraft, vehicles, or persons in distress, or amateur or CB radio and many others, the list being too screwy and involved to present here**.*

*LEGAL TIP: NO PREEMPTION OF STATE'S POWERS: States can enact their own statues should they be so bold or foolish. We reckons that the radar detector on yer automobile dashboard is subject to state regulations similar to this.*

### 47 USC 605, DISTILLED VERSION

☠ *CAN'T NOBODY HAVE NO COMMUNICATIONS INTERCEPT EQUIPMENT.*

☠ *IF YOU DO HAVE INTERCEPT EQUIPMENT, YOU CAN'T INTERCEPT NOTHIN'.*

☠ *IF YOU DO INTERCEPT SOMETHING, YOU CAN'T BENEFIT FROM IT.*

☠ *IF YOU DO INTERCEPT SOMETHING, YOU CAN'T TELL NOBODY ABOUT IT.*

☠ *IF YOU DO TELL SOMEBODY ABOUT IT, YOU CAN'T BENEFIT FROM THE TELLIN'.*

☠ *AN' HAVE A NICE DAY, Y'HEAR?*

**Note that these screwy and largely unenforceable statutes take the security onus off the person who transmits his precious information without sufficient protection. They rest the responsibility instead on anybody who happens to use a radio receiver. It is essentially the statutory and technological equivalent of permitting a**

public bulletin board, but decreeing some of the posted notes to be "strictly private" under the law. This resembles hanging a notice saying;

---

# "UNDER PENALTY OF LAW
## DO NOT READ THIS SIGN"
## (OOPS! YOU ALREADY READ IT?)

---

And so, to close this lesson, we offer the following obligatory catechism query and response.

## *Intellectual Property Crime Catechism*

### *Question #4:*

*Question: CAN WE GO TO JAIL JUST FOR LISTENING?*

*Answer: YES WE CAN! YES WE CAN! (At least if we do it electronically)*

%%%%%%%%%%%%%%%%%%%%%%%%%%%%%%%%%%%%%%%

FOOTNOTES

[1] "[Tennessee Governor] Haslam said... *he wasn't familiar with the details of the legislation...* but given the recording industry presence [in Tennessee] he favors "anything we can do to cut back" on music piracy." (Emphasis added.)
See **http://forums.anandtech.com/showthread.php?t=2169269**.

[2] *"NSA" = NATIONAL SECURITY AGENCY: Government eavesdropping outfit--an organization reputed to dwarf the CIA in both manpower and funding. According to* <u>Wikipedia</u>, *"The National Security Agency/Central Security Service (NSA/CSS) is a cryptologic intelligence agency of the United States ..."* (MOTTO: **"Radio NSA, the station that listens to you!"**)

# Intellectual Property Crime Catechism
## Lesson #5
# The Prehistoric Video-Cassette Tape and Miserably Failed Security Features Statutes

*Pirate's Rule #29: Legislation can never keep up with technology. (And technology specific legislation never works.)*

For our next lesson in intellectual property crime, we do a bit of time travel back to, among other things, the days of Video Home System (VHS) and Beta video tapes. The first statute criminalizes "workarounds" used against anti-copy systems. It makes it illegal to engineer around the copyright security features on your video tape...if you had a video tape...and it had a security feature. (Can you even *find* your VHS machine?)

This statute has loads of exceptions, however, too numerous and complex to discuss here. And on the whole, it appears that its time has largely come and gone.

If you remember the "anti-copy" technologies added to some digital recordings several years ago, then you probably also remember the disastrous damage inflicted on computer operating systems and the resultant lawsuits against the companies that foisted such ill-conceived stuff on the public. *Nuff said!*

Apple Records®, admirably appearing to have learned from observing this history, released (in late 2009) a full library of Beatles® tunes on a single thumb drive, *sans* copy prevention technologies. (Perhaps taking a little swipe at Apple Computers®, against whom there still appeared to be a bit of a trademark grudge, the thumb drive comes encased in a cute plastic apple.)

# CIRCUMVENTION OF COPYRIGHT PROTECTION SYSTEMS
## 17 USC. § 1201

**OFFENSE:**
☠ *Don't go and* **circumvent no technological measure that controls access** *to stuff protected under this title.*

☠ *Also y'all better not* **manufacture, or traffic** *in any technology, or service that primarily exists or is marketed for use in circumventing an access control measure.*

☠ *No commercially clueless clod shall* **manufacture, import, offer to the public**, *provide or otherwise traffic in any* **VHS, 8mm or Beta format analog video cassette recorder** *or camcorder unless such recorder conforms to statutorily mandated* **automatic gain control copy prevention technology**.

**PENALTIES:**
☠ *Statutory damages for each violation of not less than $200 or more than* **$2,500** *per act of circumvention, device, product, component, offer, or performance of service.*

**EXCEPTIONS:** *This prohibition don't apply to nobody who may somehow be construed to fall under the many fuzzy exemptions arbitrarily defined by several paragraphs included in the statute, but too excruciatingly detailed and mealy mouthed to address in this forum. Look it up, yerself.*

**As a little side issue to this, we must also address:**

197

# *Messin' with the Labels*

## <u>INTEGRITY OF COPYRIGHT MANAGEMENT</u>
## <u>INFORMATION</u>
## <u>17 USC Secs. 1202</u>

*OFFENSE:*

☠ *No sneakin' SOB intended to induce, enable, facilitate, or conceal copyright infringement, shall promulgate **false copyright management information**, nor distribute or import goods having false copyright management information. (This includes digital information.)*

☠ *Neither shall no such disreputable snake eyed varmint **remove or alter any copyright management information**,*

☠ *nor **distribute**, nor import for distribution, goods knowing their copyright management information has been removed or fiddled with,*

☠ *nor distribute, import for distribution, or **publicly perform** works, copies of works, or phonorecords, whilst knowing that some slick willy has messed with the copyright management information,*

☠ *if'n the situation is such that any danged fool with a lick o' sense would know that it will induce, enable, facilitate, or conceal an infringement of any copyright,*

☠ *(less'n, of course, he has some sort of leeegitimate permission or authority).*

198

*LEGAL TIP:* The term "copyright management information" means:
- ❀ The title and other identifying information
- ❀ The name of the author
- ❀ The name of the copyright owner

*LEGAL TIP::* There are a bunch of exceptions to allow for technological capabilities, government or law enforcement incapability, or excess expense, ("financial hardship") and more.

*PENALTIES:*
- ☠ Penalties are listed in the following two sections.

# *Penalties for "Bustin' the Code"*

The following two sections (1203 and 1204) assign remedies (compensations) and penalties for violation of the previous two sections (1201 and 1202). Of these next two, the first is not really a matter of criminal law. It addresses only civil remedies, not criminal penalties, for tampering with copyright protection and management systems. But, it helps us achieve a more complete appreciation of this statutory series.

# COPYRIGHT PROTECTION AND MANAGEMENTSYSTEMS
## CIVIL REMEDIES
### 17 USC. § 1203

## NON-CRIMINAL PENALTIES AND REMEDIES:
☠ *For violation of section 1201 or 1202 (above) the injured party may bring a* **civil action (suit) in United States district court.**

*The court may order:*
☠ **Injunctions** *to prevent or restrain further violation; and/or*
☠ **Impoundment** *of any device or product that was involved in a violation; and/or*
☠ *Recovery of* **court costs** *by or against any party (except the United States and officers of the United States. Now there's a cheeky immunity.).*

☠ **Attorney's fees** *to the prevailing party;*

☠ *Modification or* **destruction of any device or product involved** *in the violation.*

*The court may award:*
☠ *For violation of section 1201 or 1202 (above):* **Actual damages** *(to recover lost profits) and the profits of the violator; or*
☠ *For each violation of section 1201:* **Statutory damages** *in the sum of not less than $200 or more than $2,500 per violation; or*
☠ *For each violation of section 1202:* **Statutory damages** *in the sum of not less than $2,500 or more than $25,000.*

200

## REPEAT VIOLATIONS:

☠ For repeat violation of section 1201 or 1202 within 3 years, the court may increase the award of damages up to triple the amount that would otherwise be awarded.

## INNOCENT VIOLATIONS (as if anybody believes that);

☠ In any case in which the [apparently illiterate and clueless] violator was not aware and had no reason to believe that his acts constituted a violation, the court may reduce or remit the total award of damages.

☠ In the case of an [astoundingly unaware] nonprofit library, archives, educational institution, or public broadcasting entity, that was not aware and had no reason to believe that its acts constituted a violation the court shall remit damages.

**LEGAL TIP:** In no event shall the court impose a prior restraint on free speech or the press protected under the 1st amendment to the Constitution.

**The next section (1204) addresses purely criminal penalties. Note that it again includes the elements of "commercial advantage" or "financial gain." This is perhaps intended to put a kink in the business of intercepting law enforcement communications by criminal elements such as, oh, for example, news reporters perhaps?**

## COPYRIGHT PROTECTION AND MANAGEMENT SYSTEMS CRIMINAL PENALTIES
## 17 USC. § 1204

*OFFENSE:*

For them what tampers with anti-copy technology or cable transmission encryption in violation of sections 1201 or 1202 (above) for commercial advantage or private financial gain:

*PENALTIES:*

*FIRST OFFENSE*

☠ *Fine:* up to *$500,000* and/or imprisonment up to *5 years.*

*SECOND OR SUBSEQUENT OFFENSES*

☠ *Fine:* up to *$1,000,000* and/or prison up to *10 years.*

*EXCEPTIONS: NONPROFITS ARE EXEMPT, INCLUDING:*
☠ *Libraries*
☠ *Archives*
☠ *Educational Institutions*
☠ *Liberal Public Broadcasting Entities. (The "liberal" part is not actually in the statute. I just threw it in because their smug pseudo-intellectual bias makes me grouchy.)*

*STATUTE OF LIMITATIONS:*
☠ *5 years*

202

# *Intellectual Property Crime Catechism*
## *Question #5:*

Question:  Can we go to jail for techno-hacking on our own paid for, personal copy of a recording?

Answer:    YES WE CAN! (You can betch'er cracker jacks on it!)*

*That's yer best liberty port turnout, lubber, not yer gedunk candy corn.

# Intellectual Property Crime Catechism
## Lesson #6
# Jail Time for Copycats

## Pirates Rule #30: Copyright infringement is, no kiddin', a federal crime.
### (But then, what isn't?)

This lesson of our *Catechism of Intellectual Property Crime* addresses two statutes against plain old vanilla copyright infringement and the penalties attached. (Blimey, it took long enough to get here!) But this lesson may hit a bit close to home for many of us. It deals with music downloading and file sharing, and insanely, the associated jail time. The penalties listed are augmented by additional punishments in the statute that follows it.

## COPYRIGHT INFRINGEMENT
## 17 USC. § 506

*OFFENSE:*
&#9760; ***WILLFUL INFRINGEMENT FOR PROFIT:*** *For private financial gain, the* **reproduction or distribution**, *including by electronic means, during any 180-day period, of one or more works, which have a total retail value of more than $1,000 or the* **distribution of a work being prepared for commercial distribution by making it available on a computer network.**

*PENALTIES:*
&#9760; ***FORFEITURE AND DESTRUCTION*** *of all copies in violation and the gear used for making them.*

*OFFENSE:*
&#9760; ***FRAUDULENT COPYRIGHT NOTICE:*** *Any person who, with fraudulent intent, places on any article a notice or indication of copyright whilst knowing it to be false, or who, with fraudulent intentions, publicly distributes or imports for public distribution any article bearing such notice or indication, gits;*

*PENALTY:*
&#9760; *Fine up to $2,500.*

*OFFENSE:*
&#9760; ***FRAUDULENT REMOVAL OF COPYRIGHT NOTICE:*** *If they ketch some weasel who, with fraudulent intent, removes or alters any notice of copyright appearing on a copy of a copyrighted work, the feds generously provide;*

*PENALTY:*
&#9760; *Fine up to $2,500.*

## OFFENSE:

&#9760; **FRAUD IN COPYRIGHT APPLICATION:** *Any urchin who knowingly makes a false representation of a material fact in or in connection with an application for copyright registration wins;*

## PENALTY

&#9760; *Fine up to $2,500.*

# PLUS!

# Add-On Penalties for Truly Adamant Fans

## (Smorgasbord Selection of Criminal Copyright Infringement Penalties)

These penalties are added on to the penalties listed under 17 USC. § 506, just addressed. This statute is convoluted, incomplete, and contains at least one glaring, drafting error. Further, it is rather improperly located under Federal Statutes Chapter 113, concerning "STOLEN PROPERTY." Perhaps this is to lend credence to the nonsensical position that copyright infringement is

206

**"theft."** A quick review of the definition of **"conversion"** in **Black's Law Dictionary** will demonstrate the presumptive and misleading falsehood of this classification.[1]

## CRIMINAL COPYRIGHT INFRINGEMENT PENALTIES
## 18 USC. § 2319

### WILLFUL INFRINGEMENT FOR THE PURPOSES OF COMMERCIAL ADVANTAGE OR PRIVATE FINANCIAL GAIN

*permits:*

☠ *If the offense consists of the reproduction or distribution, during any 180-day period, of at least 10 copies of copyrighted works, having total retail value greater than $2.5 grand it earns up to 5 years in the SLAMMER and/or fined per provisions in this title.*

☠ *SUBSEQUENT OFFENSE gets the HOOSEGOW up to* **10 years** *and/or fine (per this title).*

☠ *CONSOLATION PRIZE: In any other case of willful infringement, the poor guilty bum earns a holiday BRIG TOUR of up to* **1 year** *and/or fine (as specified in this here title).*

### WILLFUL INFRINGEMENT BY REPRODUCTION OR DISTRIBUTION OF 10 OR MORE COPIES OF COPYRIGHTED WORKS

☠ *If the works have a* **total retail value of $2,500 or more**, *this earns our lucky winner a ROOM IN THE BIG HOUSE for up to* **3 years and/or fine**, *as specified in this title.*

☠ *SECOND OR SUBSEQUENT OFFENSE under this paragraph jacks the jail term up to* **6 years** *and/or a fine.*

207

## REPRODUCTION OR DISTRIBUTION OF ONE OR MORE COPIES OF COPYRIGHTED WORKS

☠ *If the works have a total retail* **value greater than $1,000**, *our contestant receives an all-expenses paid trip UP THE RIVER up to* **1 year** *and/or fine as specified in this title.*

## WILLFUL INFRINGEMENT BY DISTRIBUTION OF A WORK BEING PREPARED FOR COMMERCIAL DISTRIBUTION, BY MAKING IT AVAILABLE ON A COMPUTER NETWORK ACCESSIBLE TO MEMBERS OF THE PUBLIC

*earns:*

☠ *LUXURY LOCK-UP up to* **3 years and/or fine***;*
*or*

☠ *IN THE CAN up to* **5 years, and/or fine**, *if the offense was committed for purposes of commercial advantage or private financial gain (What other reason is there?).*

☠ **SECOND OR SUBSEQUENT OFFENSE** *sends the poor guilty bum clinkward bound for up to* **6 years** *and/or fined.*

☠ **SOME SUBSEQUENT OFFENSES** *purportedly earn more jail time for up to* **10 years and/or a fine**, *"if the offense is a second or subsequent offense* **under paragraph (2).**" *However, this is merely "purported" because, due to an apparent typographical or drafting error,* **there appears to be NO applicable "paragraph (2)."**

☠ *All offenders are required to endure a* **victim impact statement. The copyright holders, producers, hucksters and their lawyers all get a shot at the miserable malefactor.**

**As noted above, the amended statute does set minimums below which "criminality"**

208

of downloading or file sharing is not attained. But the standard is not difficult to meet. Any kid with a free afternoon can achieve it.

Just download, file share, or copy a medium capacity, hard drive solidly packed full of iTunes® and you, too, can qualify for an all-expense paid vacation in a beautifully manicured federal residential facility complete with a fully equipped gymnasium, handicraft classes, and an anger management counselor. It's easy, and after all nobody can do just one!

So, finally do we address the nitty-gritty of what hypothetically speaking the hypothetical reader may have hypothetically stored on his hypothetical laptop computer or iPhone®. We address the primary hypothetical question on everybody's hypothetical minds.

## *Intellectual Property Crime Catechism*

### *Question #6:*

*Question: "Can we go to jail for sharing music files?"*

*Answer: YES WE CAN! YES WE CAN! (Hypothetically, anyway.)*

# Intellectual Property Crime Catechism
## Lesson #7
# Cable Providers and Your Privacy

*Pirate's Rule#30: Your cable company is statutorily obligated to protect your privacy.*

Let not the reader get an impression that only little guys can get hauled into court. Corporate purveyors of audio, video, and Web-based entertainment may also find themselves in dire straits, if'n they dasn't mind their "Ps" and "Qs." This lesson conveys the penalties for cable service providers (TV, Internet, telephone) who get too loose and free with private customer information.

Since this does not involve jail time or fines, it does not strictly speaking constitute a criminal statute. But, all the same, it carries some potential penalties, and familiarity with its content may prove important. You may find it handy as weapon in a pinch.

We have intimately observed the conduct and attitudes of several cable providers in these matters. Their loyalty to customers, degrees of attention to details of customer security, and protection of customer privacy interests, vary widely.

We don't know who is best and we ain't shillin' for no particular company or nothing. But, if you have a cable provider who seems danged willing to turn over yer information to any wandering lawyer or judge on a fishing expedition, we suggest that you cut bait and find a new cable company. They probably are violating this statute and putting you an unnecessary risk.

Further, we can confide that Time Warner® appears to have notable record of pro-subscriber conduct in this arena. Giving credit where credit is due they do not hesitate to go to the mat to protect their customers against sleazy demands and abusive subpoenas. If history is any indicator, we figger that if you watch what Time Warner® does, and if you find your provider does the same as they, then you can trust yer provider is prob'ly doing right by you.

We dono why they do it. Maybe they just likes a good fight. Or maybe it's because they calculates that protecting their cable customers is good business,...because it *is*.

## CABLE PRIVACY ACT OF 1984
## 47 USC Sec. 551

### OFFENSE:

Yer **cable operator can't go and disclose none of** yer **personally identifiable information**, *and must prevent access to such information, unless:*

☠ *The subscriber (you) consents in writing;*

*or*

☠ *Such disclosure is necessary to render service to you;*

*or*

☠ *A court* <u>having the necessary jurisdiction</u> *authorizes such disclosure, and the subscriber (you) is in advance notified of such authorization,*

*or*

☠ *Such disclosure is:*

❀ *to a "cable service,"*
*and*

❀ *the subscriber (you) got an opportunity to opt out,*
*and*

❀ *certain specific viewing information is excluded (listed in the statute).*

### PENALTIES:
**Civil Action and Damages**

*Subscribers (or other such aggrieved, damaged, offended, done wrong, jilted, or abused, victims) may bring a civil action (e.g. "sue the scurvy dogs") to enforce this prohibition against disclosure, and may recover:*

☠ *actual damages in compensation,* **not less than $100 per day or $1000**, *whichever is higher;*
*and*

&#9763; **punitive damages** (forfeiture of more money, just to teach
'em a lesson);
and
&#9763; **attorney's fees** (for yer own attorney, not theirs).

## Intellectual Property Crime Catechism
## Question #7:

Question: *"Can cable service providers go to jail for sharing your private information?"*

Answer: *Well, no, not jail really. But they sho' nuff can git squeezed for some serious coin if'n they does you wrong.*

# Intellectual Property Crime Catechism
## Lesson #8
# No Jail Time for
# "Patent Pirates"

## Pirate's Rule #31: Patent infringement ain't no crime!

The final lesson of our CATECHISM OF INTELLECTUAL PROPERTY CRIME is that unlike copyrights, trade secrets, and trademarks, patents are enforced entirely under civil law. *There are no criminal statutes to bolster them.* When it comes to the serious business of protecting the really valuable national treasures, the products of our great technological innovators, inventors are left on their own. Concisely said, we can quote no criminal statutes, for thar AIN'T no criminal patent infringement laws.

# Intellectual Property Crime Catechism
## Question #8:

Question: "Can we go to jail for ripping off the patent for the next new:
- ☠ AIDS vaccine
- ☠ Cancer cure
- ☠ Flying car
- ☠ Petroleum-free fuel
- ☠ Clean nuclear reactor
- ☠ Hair dressing device
- ☠ Snot resistant nose whistle
  or
- ☠ Any other patented invention?

Answer: No. Negative. Indubitably, categorically not. Nuh uh.

Although, Mis-tah Cris-chen, they can have ye gaoled for nicking movies, books, newspaper articles, music, jingles, photos, logos, or tartan tattooed on yer laird's lumbar, there are *no* criminal penalties for pirating patents! No keelhauling. No hangin' from the yard arm at sunrise. No lashin' with the cat-o-nine-tails. No stocks. No three days in the brig on bread and water. *Nothing!* Shiver what's left o' me timbers, ye won't even git yer shore leave canceled or weekend liberty card pulled!

So, thar be no need for nobody to steer for the coast of Somalia for piratical roving. Patent pirates have plenty of happy hunting grounds anytime, anywhere, and right at home!

*End of Catechism*

# Appendix II
# Tactical Weapons Matrix

# Tactical Weapons Matrix

As a modern combat officer at sea I had a broad and complex selection of weapons at my disposal. The possible combinations were vast and the potential tactical situations always dynamic. Constant re-evaluation of weapons employment, especially in the heat of battle, was essential to selection of the most appropriate "tools" (weapons).

So every shipboard weaponeer created and memorized a "weapons matrix." This was sort of a thumbnail crib sheet that laid out the essential parameters of each weapon. It was vitally useful in helping the harried fighter revise his tactics "on the fly."

Similarly the following tactical matrix will help you compare your defensive and offensive options with respect to the intellectual property tools at your disposal. Mix this information with some practical business sense, and be creative.

Particularly note the overlaps for many subjects, such as those between copyrights, design patents, and trademarks. Ornamental creations may be covered by any or all of these protections. Also note carefully the humongous differences in terms of protection and the vast variation in cost. ("Low" cost means as little as a few hundred dollars. "Medium" may mean as low as two or three thousand dollars...or a bit more. "High" does not have a top end limit.)

Further with respect to copyrights, just figure that for practical purposes *copyrights last forever*. Practically speakin', me hearties, we hardly calculates that Congress will let any Disney® Productions lose copyright protection. So go *Pirates of the Caribbean*®, so go we all. Armorer, break out the weapons!

# INTELLECTUAL PROPERTY TACTICAL WEAPONS MATRIX

| SUBJECT | PROTECTION AVAILABLE* | PROTECTION PERIOD | COST |
|---|---|---|---|
| DEVICE, SYSTEM, PRODUCT, or METHOD | UTILITY PATENT*** | 20 YEARS FROM DATE OF FILING | HIGH ## |
| COMPUTER PROGRAM | UTILITY PATENT*** <br> COPYRIGHT**** | 20 YEARS FROM DATE OF FILING <br> LIFETIME OF AUTHOR, PLUS 70 YEARS (WITH EXCEPTIONS) | HIGH ## <br> LOW |
| LIVING PLANT INVENTION | PLANT PATENT*** | 20 YEARS FROM DATE OF FILING | HIGH ## |
| AESTHETIC DESIGN (2 DIMENSIONAL OR 3 DIMENSIONAL) | DESIGN PATENT*** <br> COPYRIGHT**** <br> TRADEMARK or SERVICE MARK** <br> TRADEDRESS | 14 YEARS FROM DATE OF ISSUE <br> LIFETIME OF AUTHOR, PLUS 70 YEARS (WITH EXCEPTIONS) <br> FOREVER. CONTINUOUS USE REQUIRED.# <br> FOREVER. CONTINUOUS USE REQUIRED.# | MEDIUM <br> LOW <br> MEDIUM <br> MEDIUM |
| ARTWORK / FINE ART (2 DIMENSIONAL or 3 DIMENSIONAL) | DESIGN PATENT*** <br> COPYRIGHT**** <br> TRADEMARK or SERVICE MARK** <br> TRADEDRESS | 14 YEARS FROM DATE OF ISSUE <br> LIFETIME OF AUTHOR, PLUS 70 YEARS (WITH EXCEPTIONS) <br> FOREVER. CONTINUOUS USE REQUIRED.# <br> FOREVER. CONTINUOUS USE REQUIRED.# | MEDIUM <br> LOW <br> MEDIUM <br> MEDIUM |
| PHOTOGRAPH or AUDIO RECORDING or VIDEO RECORDING | COPYRIGHT**** | LIFETIME OF AUTHOR, PLUS 70 YEARS (WITH EXCEPTIONS) | LOW |
| BOOK, ARTICLE, ESSAY POETRY, SHEET MUSIC, BROCHURE, MANUAL | COPYRIGHT**** | LIFETIME OF AUTHOR, PLUS 70 YEARS (WITH EXCEPTIONS) | LOW |
| TRADE NAME or SYMBOL | TRADEMARK or SERVICE MARK** | FOREVER. CONTINUOUS USE REQUIRED # | MEDIUM |
| BUSINESS SLOGAN | TRADEMARK or SERVICE MARK** | FOREVER. CONTINUOUS USE REQUIRED # | MEDIUM |
| TRADE SECRET | STATE and FEDERAL LAW <br> NON-DISCLOSURE AGREEMENTS | FOREVER. SO LONG AS AGGRESSIVELY GUARDED <br> AS INDICATED IN THE AGREEMENT | LOW <br> LOW |

* Note many overlaps.
** Registration available at state and federal levels.
*** Federal only. May be filed or prosecuted only by attorney or agent registered to practice before the *United States Patent and Trademark Office* (or pro se).
**** Criminal sanctions also available.
# Registration, available, but not required, is renewable so long as use continues.
## Significant maintenance fees due every 3.5 years

# *Appendix III*
# *Example Protections*
# *Tactically Employed*

❀    1946 AIRFRAME protected by UTILITY PATENT

❀    1949 PROPELLER protected by DESIGN PATENT

❀    1939 aircraft NAME ("Ercoupe") protected by TRADEMARK

❀    2010 aircraft PHOTO protected by COPYRIGHT

❀    1953 ~~PIRATE~~ PILOT protected by GOD'S SENSE OF HUMOR

# About the Author

Patent Attorney David Winters is a uniquely qualified authority in practical piracy. Originally a crisp United States Naval Academy man pursuing a squeaky-clean career at sea, he found himself seduced by the dark arts of codes and cyphers. Thus turned, he was dispatched abroad to defend against spies, snoops, hackers, and other shadowy scalawags, across far-flung oceans and continents.* Decades later, he retired his Navy sword, expanded and went freelance, capitalizing on his cloak and dagger** background in Europe and Asia. ***

Having begun his slide down this proverbial "slippery slope," our pirate inevitably sank to the point of admission to practice before the bar of law. But all was for the best. His combination of pragmatic knowhow and savvy counsel perfectly fit the world of intellectual property, and produced a stupendous family of successful clients.

%%%%%%%%%%%%%%%%%%%%%%%%%%%%%%%%%%%%%%%

FOOTNOTES

* During this period he operated sans uniform out of London from whence he also had the privilege of leading special operations missions in [*significant pause*] unusual locations. Think James Bond, except without the good looks, charm, or... sigh... inexhaustible sources of untaxed cash.

** Well, really more cloak than dagger.

*** His passports, of various colors, vaguely termed him a "Specialist in International Services." To his disappointment, there was no classification flatly titled "International Man of Mystery."

221

# *Reviewers' Comments*

*****(Five Stars) **Insightful!!! Excellent work by the author to simplify concepts in an educational and humorous way. Easy to read, finished it in a weekend.** *(Ali Baba, AMAZON reviewer)*

*****(Five Stars) **Amazing facts done with amazing humor... He kept me laughing the whole time I was learning!** *(Jay Perdue, inventor and entrepreneur)*

**... an entertaining read! ... a bounty of information in an easily digestible, humorous format.** *(Nashville Bar Journal).*

**...quirky and definitely irreverent...*The Pirates Guide* will entertain and provide food for thought**. *(IP, Tennessee Bar online magazine.)*

**It would be wise for many of you to consider buying this book... Remember, forewarned is forearmed.** *(MENSA BULLETIN, The Magazine of American Mensa)*

Made in the USA
Charleston, SC
06 January 2014